BUSINESS ENGLISH
THIRD EDITION

Jeanne Reed, M.Ed.

Former Director of Business Education
Detroit Public Schools
Detroit, Michigan

A Gregg Text-Kit for Adult Education

D1402761

Gregg Division/McGraw-Hill Book Company

New York / St. Louis / Dallas / San Francisco / Auckland / Bogotá
Düsseldorf / Johannesburg / London / Madrid / Mexico / Montreal
New Delhi / Panama / Paris / São Paulo / Singapore / Sydney
Tokyo / Toronto

Contents

808
R

117794

BUSINESS ENGLISH, Third Edition

Copyright © 1978, 1972, 1966 by McGraw-Hill, Inc. All Rights Reserved. Printed in the United States of America. No part of this publication may be reproduced, stored in a retrieval system, or transmitted, in any form or by any means, electronic, mechanical, photocopying, recording, or otherwise, without the prior written permission of the publisher.

34567890 BABA 78765432109

ISBN 0-07-051497-6

To the Student

The ability to communicate is basic to success in the business world. Any career that you choose will require you to communicate frequently, and the more effectively you can do so, the better your chances for job success will be. The reason is simple: The person who can write a memo that clearly solves a problem, a letter that soothes an angry customer or a report that gives all the necessary information (without unnecessary details) is saving time and money for the company—and is probably gaining new customers along the way. Obviously, such a person is valuable in today's business world. Just as obviously, business English is the key to preparing effective memos, letters, and reports.

But what is **business** English? How does it differ from the English most of us use? Put simply, business English is the practical application of our language to the needs of the business world. Business English emphasizes the correct, simple, tactful expression of ideas both in speaking and in writing.

A Plan to Improve Speaking and Writing Skills

Your *Business English* text-kit includes five parts, each designed to aid you in a specific way:

1. *Business English*—your basic text. At the beginning of each unit in the text, you will find an objective for your study of that unit. The objective is followed by one or more points you will need to remember from previous units. Then, basic principles of sentence structure, grammar, punctuation, and business usage are presented briefly, step by step and are followed by examples that will help you understand how to apply each principle.

    Following each principle or two presented, you will find a few practice sentences that will help you check your understanding. You are shown the correct answers for these sentences so that you can determine immediately whether you are ready to go on to the next principle.

2. Self-Checks—a pad of practice materials to check your understanding of each unit of the textbook. These Self-Checks provide further practice in applying the principles in the unit. In addition, every Self-Check contains a Vocabulary Pitfall section. This section deals with special problems: overused words and expressions, words that sound alike or nearly alike but have different meanings, and so on. Paying attention to these common pitfalls in written and spoken English will help you to make a marked improvement in your ability to communicate effectively.

3. Self-Check Key—a booklet that gives you the answers to the Self-Checks. By comparing your answers to the correct answers, you can determine immediately which principles you understand and can apply without difficulty and which principles need further study and practice.

4. Review Sheets—a pad of additional exercises that help you to (a) check once more your understanding of the principles studied in a particular unit

and (b) review principles you have studied in previous units. The instructor will check each Review Sheet before you go on to the next unit.

5. **Surveys** — a set of materials to help evaluate your progress in understanding language-usage principles. Your instructor will assign the Surveys at various times during the course.

Thus the text-kit materials give you repeated opportunities to learn and to apply the basic principles of business English.

Helpful Hints

Accomplishing the goals of effective communication will not be difficult if you make sure you understand each principle that is presented. After studying the basic principles, try them out in the practice exercises, and then apply them as you speak and write each day.

It will also be helpful to listen to the sound of grammatically correct expressions. When the sound of a correct form becomes fixed in your mind, you can speak and write that form correctly without having to stop and think about the rule that applies.

Your *Business English* text-kit provides the principles for you to understand, to practice, and to apply. Listen and observe to fix the sound and structure of correct expressions in your mind and then use these forms in your daily speaking and writing.

The Sentence

YOUR OBJECTIVE
To recognize a sentence and see it as a framework for expressing thoughts.

WHY?
You must know the sentence and its structure to learn in later units the correct grammar and punctuation skills needed for clear communication.

What a Sentence Is

A sentence is a group of words expressing a complete thought. The words must be able to stand alone and express a complete thought; otherwise the words are not a sentence. One easy way to check for a complete thought is to apply this guide: *no sense, no sentence.*

A report of the annual meeting is due today.

This group of words is a sentence because it expresses a complete thought. The statement has everything needed to make sense; nothing is missing.

When the report is completed.

Does this group of words make sense? Do the words express a complete thought? No. The reader needs to know more. What will happen "When the report is completed"? Will it be duplicated? mailed? filed? Something is missing; the group of words is not a sentence.

Practice

Study these groups of words to determine which are sentences and which are not. Remember, no sense, no sentence. *If you have any trouble, look at the key at the right.*

1. Many new desks are made of metal   1. Yes
2. A time schedule will be posted tomorrow   2. Yes
3. In regard to your letter of March 7   3. No
4. When the current inventory is used   4. No
5. A telephone operator is on duty all day   5. Yes

Subject and Predicate

Every sentence has two basic parts—a subject and a predicate. Your ability to recognize the subject and the predicate in a sentence will help you understand many basic English principles.

The *complete subject* of a sentence is a word or a group of words that shows *who is speaking, who is spoken to,* or *the person or thing spoken about.* The *complete predicate* is the rest of the sentence. It says something about the subject—*what the subject does, what is done to the subject,* or *what state of being the subject is in.*

I will complete the report this afternoon. *I* is the complete subject—the person speaking. The complete predicate is *will complete the report this afternoon.*

You are an accurate typist. *You* is the complete subject—the person spoken to. The rest of the sentence is the complete predicate.

The artist who drew the illustration is a talented person. *The artist who drew the illustration* is the complete subject of the sentence—the person spoken about. The complete predicate is *is a talented person.*

Four file cabinets have been moved to the warehouse. *Four file cabinets* is the complete subject—the things spoken about. The complete predicate is *have been moved to the warehouse.*

Note: Some sentences have unexpressed subjects; the actual subjects are understood. For example, in the sentence *Type three copies,* the word *You* is understood as the subject; thus *(You) type three copies.*

Practice

Find the complete subject in the following sentences.

1. New typewriters were purchased last year.
2. Examinations are to be given tomorrow.
3. Ms. Harris will start work next week.
4. The figures are to be typed in three columns.
5. Please order two dozen ribbons.
6. I must learn to proofread carefully.
7. All employees must accept responsibility.
8. We will pay the bill by November 30.

1. **New typewriters**
2. **Examinations**
3. **Ms. Harris**
4. **The figures**
5. **You** (understood)
6. **I**
7. **All employees**
8. **We**

Simple and Compound Subjects

If you can identify simple subjects and compound subjects, you will be better able to recognize many common writing errors. A *simple subject* is the single most important element in the complete subject. A *compound subject* consists of two or more equally important words that are part of the complete subject and that are joined by the conjunction *and, or,* or *nor.* Remember that the subject shows *who is speaking, who is spoken to,* or *the person or thing spoken about.*

To find the simple subject, look for the most important word in the complete subject.

Our new bookkeeper will work in the Dayton office. The complete subject is *Our new bookkeeper. Bookkeeper,* the most important word in the complete subject, is the simple subject.

The woman in the blue dress is a new employee. What is the complete subject? It is *The woman in the blue dress.* What is the simple subject? To recognize it, you must find the most important single word. That word is *woman.*

If the complete subject contains two or more equally important words joined by a conjunction, the sentence has a compound subject.

Mary and Phillip, both excellent tennis players, have entered the tournament. The complete subject is *Mary and Phillip, both excellent tennis players.* Two equally important words—*Mary* and *Phillip*—form the subject; these words are joined by the conjunction *and.* The sentence therefore has a compound subject, *Mary and Phillip.*

The debits and credits in the trial balance must be equal. What is the complete subject? It is *The debits and credits in the trial balance.* What is the most important element in the complete subject? In this case it consists of more than one word—*debits and credits;* therefore, the sentence has a compound subject.

💋 Practice

Identify the simple or the compound subject in each of the following sentences.

1. Jean Duff is learning to program the new computer.

   1. **Jean Duff** Simple.

2. Mario Manos and Ruth Bennett will attend the advertising meeting.

   2. **Mario Manos and Ruth Bennett** Compound.

3. The stencil duplicator or the fluid duplicator may be used for copying reports.

   3. **stencil duplicator or fluid duplicator** Compound.

4. See if Mr. James has left his office.

   4. **You** Understood.

5. The machine equipped with tape is a listing device.

   5. **machine** Simple.

6. The tone of a person's voice could arouse customer resentment.

   6. **tone** Simple.

Normal and Inverted Sentence Order

A sentence is in normal order when the complete subject precedes the predicate. If the first word or words in the sentence are not the subject, the sentence is in inverted order. As you continue your study, you will find it important to be able to distinguish the subject from the predicate no matter what the sentence order is. Normal word order, however, produces stronger, more direct sentences that you will find better suited to most business needs.

The manager of our department announced a price increase. Since the complete subject (*The manager of our department*) precedes the predicate, the sentence is in normal order.

Between here and the warehouse the package disappeared. Here we are talking about *the package*, which is the complete subject. Since the complete subject does not precede the complete predicate, the sentence is in inverted order. Changed to normal order, it reads: *The package disappeared between here and the warehouse.*

Whom have you and Sandra asked to work with you? This sentence is in inverted order, as most questions are. You may change inverted order to normal order by rearranging the words so that the complete subject is written first, followed by the complete predicate. Normal order is as follows: *You have asked whom to work with you?*

Although changing a question into normal order may make the sentence sound odd or may alter the meaning slightly, do not be concerned. Changing the order merely helps you to find the subject.

⚙ Practice

The following sentences are in inverted order. Change each to normal order.

1. At the present time we are not raising prices.

   1. We are not raising prices at the present time.

2. Rushing out of the elevator came a crowd of tired athletes and their coaches.

   2. A crowd of tired athletes and their coaches came rushing out of the elevator.

3. When the new files were delivered, the secretary was on vacation.

   3. The secretary was on vacation when the new files were delivered.

4. To the beginning worker, the first day on the job is likely to be confusing.

   4. The first day on the job is likely to be confusing to the beginning worker.

5. Soon after their arrival the telephone began to ring.

   5. The telephone began to ring soon after their arrival.

⚎ Assignment

Check your understanding of the sentence as the framework for expressing thoughts by doing Self-Check 1; then use the Self-Check Key to evaluate your work. In addition, complete Review Sheet 1, and turn it in to your instructor for scoring.

Verbs—Part 1

YOUR OBJECTIVE

To recognize verbs and verb phrases and know their use for correct and forceful expression.

REMEMBER ...

A sentence is composed of a subject and a predicate, and the complete predicate says something about the subject.

The predicate follows the complete subject when the sentence is written in normal order.

The essential element of every predicate is a verb or verb phrase.

What a Verb Does

A *verb* serves the same purpose in a sentence as the motor serves in a car. Without the motor or the verb, neither the car nor the sentence goes anywhere—nothing happens. For example, examine the following groups of words, which do *not* include verbs:

The cleaning fluid on the floor.
Mary Avery her foot.
Most file drawers easily.

Did the cleaning fluid *spill* on the floor? Did Mary Avery *bruise* her foot? Do most file drawers *close* easily? When you supply these or other verbs, the message is clear and something happens.

The verbs supplied in the preceding sentences all represent action. Other verbs may express a condition or a state of being.

The office manager says she *feels* pleased with the work. Condition.
Mrs. Cortez *is* the secretary. State of being.

Practice

Can you locate the verbs in the following sentences? If the verb is missing, supply one that gives the sentence meaning.

1. The lounge was yellow.

2. She the necessary file folders.

1. was

2. She (**found, located**) the necessary file folders.

3. Mr. Johnson his overdue account.

4. All tags show the prices clearly marked.

5. The messenger the mail.

3. Mr. Johnson (paid, neglected) his overdue account.

4. show

5. The messenger (brought, delivered, lost) the mail.

Verb Phrases

In some cases two or more verbs are grouped together to form the predicate of a sentence. This grouping of verbs is called a *verb phrase*. For example:

Mrs. Marino *is staying* in Atlanta.
Your order *will be mailed* tomorrow.

A verb phrase consists of a *main* or *principal* verb plus one or more *helping* or *auxiliary* verbs. The last word in a verb phrase is always the main or principal verb. As you study verb phrases, you will notice that some verbs may be used as main verbs in some sentences and as helping verbs in others. Here is a list of the commonly used helpers:

be, am, is, are, was, were, being, been, have, has, had
can, could, shall, should, will, would, may, might, must

These helpers are often combined as follows:

has been	will have	may have been
is being	can have	could have been
might be	should be	must have been

The following sentences show how helping verbs are used with main verbs to make verb phrases:

Mr. Pittman *has been working* at the reception desk. The verb phrase is *has been working*. *Working*, the last verb, is the main verb; *has* and *been* are helpers.

He *will find* many ways to save money. Verb phrase, *will find*; main verb, *find*; helper, *will*.

Mr. Jamison *was* there. There is no verb phrase in this sentence. The verb is *was*. In this sentence *was* is the main verb.

Could Ms. Kent *have seen* the office manager? Verb phrase, *could have seen*; main verb, *seen*; helpers, *could* and *have*. (Remember to change a question into normal order to identify the subject and predicate.)

What film *will be shown* at the marketing conference? Verb phrase, *will be shown*; main verb, *shown*; helpers, *will* and *be*.

✏️ Practice

Select the verb phrase, the main verb, and the helping verb or verbs in each of the following sentences.

1. A department head should keep up-to-date personnel files.

1. should keep Verb phrase.
   keep Main verb.
   should Helping verb.

2. Have you answered all pertinent questions?

2. have answered Verb phrase.
   answered Main verb.
   have Helping verb.

3. All reports could have been completed by June 30.

3. **could have been completed** Verb phrase.
   completed Main verb.
   could, have, been Helping verbs.

4. The staff is failing in its efforts to maintain production standards.

4. **is failing** Verb phrase.
   failing Main verb.
   is Helping verb.

5. The offices will be moved by next month.

5. **will be moved** Verb phrase.
   will, be Helping verbs.

Compound Predicates

Just as a sentence may have a compound subject, so may a sentence have a compound predicate. A compound predicate consists of two or more verbs or verb phrases of equal importance joined by a conjunction.

Price walked to the door and held it open. The complete predicate is *walked to the door and held it open;* the compound predicate is *walked and held.*

Miss Rubin will arrive at ten and should complete the work by four. The most important elements in the predicate are the two verb phrases *will arrive* and *should complete;* thus the sentence has a compound predicate.

The auditor will check your records and submit the necessary reports. Note that the compound predicate is made up of two verb phrases; but since the helper *will* applies to the two main verbs *check* and *submit, will* is not repeated with the second verb, *submit.*

✎ Practice

In each of the following sentences, identify the complete predicate. Then tell whether it contains a verb phrase or a compound predicate.

1. The meeting is scheduled for 10 a.m. tomorrow.

1. **is scheduled for 10 a.m. tomorrow** Complete predicate.
   is scheduled Verb phrase.

2. Flight 420 departed ten minutes late but arrived on time.

2. **departed ten minutes late but arrived on time** Complete predicate.
   departed but arrived Compound predicate.

3. A customer called yesterday and canceled her order.

3. **called yesterday and canceled her order** Complete predicate.
   called and canceled Compound predicate.

4. Why not complete and mail the enclosed application today?

4. The subject *you* is understood in this sentence; therefore, the entire sentence as written is the complete predicate.
   complete and mail Compound predicate.

5. Several bids have been received.

5. **have been received** Complete predicate and verb phrase.

Verb Tenses

Verbs have different forms that are used to indicate the *time*, or *tense*, of the action, condition, or state of being that exists. Each verb has four principal parts from which all its tenses are formed.

PRESENT	walk	investigate
PAST	walked	investigated
PAST PARTICIPLE	walked	investigated
PRESENT PARTICIPLE	walking	investigating

The *present* form of the verb is used to express present tense or to make a statement that is true at all times. The present form is also used with the helping verbs *shall* and *will* to show future tense.

The receptionists *greet* all callers. Present.
The president *will greet* new employees. Future.

The *past* form of the verb is used to express past tense.

Maria *greeted* her old friend. Past.
One typist *finished* his work by noon. Past.

The *past participle* is used with *have, has, had,* and other helping verbs to form the so-called "perfect tenses"—present perfect, past perfect, and future perfect.

The Texas Textile Company *has placed* a large order. Present perfect.
He *had walked* to work. Past perfect.
Mr. Jackson *will have finished* his report by Friday. Future perfect.

Remember, the past tense form of a verb never uses a helping verb. Also remember that the past participle form must *always* have a helping verb.

The *present participle* is used to form the progressive tenses. These tenses are called *progressive* to indicate that something is *in progress.* They suggest a continuing action or state of being in the present, past, or future. The present participle is used with some form of the verb *to be* to create the progressive tenses.

He *is walking* to work. Present progressive.
They *were waiting* to read his new manuscript. Past progressive.
Sally *will be flying* to Bermuda next month. Future progressive.

🕪 Practice

Find the verbs or verb phrases in the following sentences. What tense is each one?

1. The two young men worked until midnight.   1. **worked**   Past tense.

2. Our baseball team has played four games.   2. **has played**   Present perfect.

3. The team is competing again today.

4. Dr. Cruz works in this building.

5. Who will print the monthly bulletin?

6. Joan had often asked to help.

3. **is competing** Present progressive.

4. **works** Present.

5. **will print** Future.

6. **had asked** Past perfect.

Regular and Irregular Verbs

Verbs are classified as *regular* or *irregular* depending on the way their past and past participle forms are constructed. Most verbs are *regular,* like those illustrated in the previous paragraphs—a *d* or an *ed* is added to the present form to make the past and past participle forms.

PRESENT	walk	illustrate	save	gather
PAST	walked	illustrated	saved	gathered
PAST PARTICIPLE	walked	illustrated	saved	gathered

The principal parts of *regular* verbs do not cause many problems in written or spoken English. However, there is some tendency to omit the *ed* from the past and past participle forms. The writer and the speaker should give special attention to adding the *ed* in both the past tense and those tenses formed with the past participle.

The family save**d** 5 percent of their earnings. Not *the family save . . . .*
We have check**ed** the entire budget. Not *we have check . . . .*

The past tense and past participle of *irregular verbs* are formed in various ways. Frequently, part of the basic word is changed, and sometimes a completely different word is used. Errors in the use of irregular verbs occur so often that these verbs require special study. For example:

PRESENT	begin	see	speak	go	write
PAST	began	saw	spoke	went	wrote
PAST PARTICIPLE	begun	seen	spoken	gone	written

The three important forms of the most common irregular verbs appear in the list on page 10. There is no substitute for memorizing these forms. The present participle form is not included there. However, it is never irregular; it is always formed by adding an *ing* to the root verb.

✪ Practice

Find the errors in verb formation in the following sentences. Add a helping verb or change the verb form in order to correct the sentences.

1. Miss Munoz done much to improve office procedures.

1. did, has done

2. The salesperson seen an error on the order.

2. saw

3. I have went to an employment agency.

3. gone

PRESENT	PAST	PAST PARTICIPLE
begin	began	begun
bid (to command)	bade	bidden *or* bid
bid (to offer to pay)	bid	bid
bite	bit	bitten
blow	blew	blown
break	broke	broken
bring	brought	brought
burst	burst	burst
catch	caught	caught
choose	chose	chosen
come	came	come
do	did	done
draw	drew	drawn
drink	drank	drunk
drive	drove	driven
eat	ate	eaten
fall	fell	fallen
fight	fought	fought
flee	fled	fled
fly	flew	flown
forget	forgot	forgotten *or* forgot
freeze	froze	frozen
get	got	got *or* gotten
give	gave	given
go	went	gone
grow	grew	grown
hang (a person)	hanged	hanged
hang (a picture)	hung	hung
hide	hid	hidden
know	knew	known
lay (put, place)	laid (*not* layed)	laid (*not* layed)
leave	left	left
lie (recline)	lay	lain
pay	paid (*not* payed)	paid (*not* payed)
ride	rode	ridden
ring	rang	rung
rise	rose	risen
run	ran	run
see	saw	seen
set	set	set
shake	shook	shaken
sit	sat	sat
speak	spoke	spoken
steal	stole	stolen
strike	struck	struck
take	took	taken
tear	tore	torn
throw	threw	thrown
wear	wore	worn
write	wrote	written

4. The patient was laying down in the clinic.   4. lying

5. He frequently has drank a quart of milk at lunchtime.   5. has drunk

6. Mr. Carver was drove by his fiery ambition.   6. was driven

7. The newsletters were ran on the offset machine.   7. were run

8. Some mail was deliver early today.   8. delivered

Infinitives

The basic form of a verb preceded by *to—to fly, to eat, to forget, to be—*is called an *infinitive.* Whenever possible, careful writers do not "split" an infinitive by using other words between *to* and the verb.

He was asked *to quickly make* 25 copies. *To quickly make* is a split infinitive. The sentence could be improved as follows: *He was asked to make 25 copies quickly.*

Is this rain going *to ever stop?* *To ever stop* is a split infinitive. The sentence should be corrected to read: *Is this rain ever going to stop?*

✷ Practice

Identify the split infinitives in the following sentences. How would you reword the sentences to avoid the awkwardness?

1. To more thoroughly understand the problem, I took time to listen to their complaints.

   1. **To understand the problem more thoroughly, I took time to listen to their complaints.**

2. The mechanic was asked to thoroughly clean each machine.

   2. **The mechanic was asked to clean each machine thoroughly.**

3. Stenographers are expected to correctly spell all dictated words.

   3. **Stenographers are expected to spell correctly . . . . (Or . . . to spell all dictated words correctly.)**

4. Your duty will be to eventually correct billing errors.

   4. **Eventually your duty will be to correct . . . . (Or Your duty will eventually be to correct . . . .)**

5. The manager reminds sales personnel to always be courteous.

   5. **The manager reminds sales personnel to be always courteous. (Or . . . to be courteous always.)**

✸ Assignment

Check your understanding of verb tense and verb formations by doing Self-Check 2; then use the Self-Check Key to evaluate your work. In addition, complete Review Sheet 2, and turn it in to your instructor for scoring.

Verbs–Part 2

YOUR OBJECTIVE

To identify (1) being verbs, (2) transitive verbs, and (3) intransitive verbs, so that you will know the verb principles necessary to use pronouns correctly.

REMEMBER . . .

Every sentence must have a verb or verb phrase that shows the action, condition, or state of being of the subject.

The forms, or parts, of verbs are used to show time or tense.

The forms, or parts, of some verbs are made in a regular manner; of others, in an irregular manner.

Being Verbs

You learned in Unit 2 that verbs show action or express a condition or a state of being. Mostly you studied about action verbs and learned that some verb tenses are formed in a regular manner, others in an irregular way. Now you will learn about *being* verbs.

Be is the most commonly used *being* verb, and it is the most irregular. A few other verbs, such as *seem, appear,* and *taste,* are considered *being* verbs when they can be replaced by forms of the verb *be* (you will learn more about these verbs in Unit 11). *Be* has these eight forms:

be	The basic (infinitive) form	He will be here.
am	Singular, present tense; used only with *I*	I am here.
is	Singular, present tense	Mary is here.
are	Plural, present tense	We, you, they are here.
was	Singular, past tense	I was here. Mary was here.
were	Plural, past tense	We, you, they were here.
being	Present participle; used with other forms of *be*	She is being tactful.
been	Past participle; used with one or more helpers	He has been here.

You will recall that some verbs may be main verbs in one sentence and helping verbs in another. For example, a form of *be* is a *being* verb only when it is used as the main verb—the last verb in a verb phrase or a verb by itself; otherwise, it is a *helping* verb.

Ms. Henry *was* in her office. *Was* is the only verb; thus it is the main verb.
The accounting department *was moved. Moved* is the main verb; *was* is the helper.

The new salesperson *could have been* number one in the country. *Been* is the last or main verb in the verb phrase *could have been*; thus it is a *being* verb, the main verb.

The letters *have been filed*. *Been* is a helping verb, not a *being* verb, in this sentence. The main verb, always the last in a verb phrase, is *filed*.

◐ Practice

Identify the verbs or verb phrases in the following sentences. Which words are being *verbs? Which are* helping *verbs?*

1. That desk is the only one already in use.

   1. **is** A *being* verb.

2. Ms. Gallo is applying for a new position.

   2. **is applying** *Is* is a helper; *applying*, the main verb.

3. The chart will be one to show miles converted to kilometers.

   3. **will be** *Will* is a helper; *be*, the main or *being* verb.

4. The treasurer's reports have been read and filed after every meeting.

   4. **have been read and filed** *Have* and *been* are helpers; *read* and *filed* are main verbs.

5. Next to our former office building were several small warehouses.

   5. **were** A *being* verb.

6. His check should have been in the mail yesterday.

   6. **should have been** *Should* and *have* are helpers; *been*, the main or *being* verb.

Transitive and Intransitive Verbs

A *transitive* verb is one that has an object; an *intransitive* verb is one that does not have an object. The *object* is the receiver or the result of the action expressed by the verb. Thus if there is an object—a receiver or a result of the action—the sentence contains a transitive verb.

Many voters *wrote* letters opposing the proposition. *Voters* is the subject; *wrote* is the verb; *letters* is the object, the result of the action expressed by the verb *wrote*. Therefore, *wrote* is a transitive verb.

The visitor *placed* Pat in an embarrassing position. *Visitor* is the subject; *placed* is the transitive verb; *Pat* is the object, the receiver of the action expressed by the verb *placed*.

To determine whether a verb is transitive, ask "What?" or "Whom?" after the verb. In the first sentence above, for example, *letters* answers the question "Wrote what?" In the second, *Pat* answers the question "Placed whom?" Therefore, in each sentence, the verb is transitive.

In other sentences, the verb may have no object—no receiver or result of the action named by the verb. In such cases, the verb is intransitive.

Thelma *stayed* at the office. Since the verb *stayed* has no object (there is no answer to the question "What?" or "Whom?"), the verb is intransitive.

Joe *arrived* early this morning. *Arrived* is an intransitive verb.

There are two exceptions to the "What?" or "Whom?" test, both of which involve *being* verbs: (1) Whenever the main verb in a sentence is a *being* verb—*were, seems, will be,* etc.—that verb is *always intransitive,* because it cannot have an object. (2) Whenever the main verb is a past participle with one of the *being* verbs as a helper—*was finished, has been hired, might be found, is driven,* etc.—that verb is *always transitive,* because the subject is the receiver or the result of the action of the verb.

> After the training course, you *should be* more efficient. *Be,* the main verb, is a *being* verb; *should* is a helper. Because a *being* verb cannot have an object, *should be* is intransitive.
>
> The contract *should have been sent* last week. *Sent* is a past participle. The *being* verb *been* is a helper. *Should have been sent* is transitive because the subject, *contract,* is the receiver of the action of the verb.
>
> Tom *was* not *following* as closely as we expected. Although the *being* verb *was* is a helper, the main verb is not a past participle (it is a present participle). Because there is no answer to "Was following what?" or to "Was following whom?" the verb is intransitive.

⚡ Practice

Determine whether the verbs in these sentences are transitive or intransitive. Use the "What?" or "Whom?" test, and watch for the exceptions involving being verbs and past participles.

1. Juan found a mistake in the debit amount.

   1. **Transitive** *Found* is the verb; *mistake* is the object.

2. All our posting was completed early today.

   2. **Transitive** *Was completed* is the verb phrase, consisting of a past participle with a form of *be* as a helper. Always transitive.

3. Did you receive a check with the order?

   3. **Transitive** *Did receive* is the verb phrase; *check* is the object.

4. Competition among auto manufacturers seems extremely keen.

   4. **Intransitive** *Seems* is a *being* verb.

5. Bad grooming eliminated the applicant from serious consideration.

   5. **Transitive** *Eliminated* is the verb; *applicant* is the object.

6. All accounts should have been audited every month.

   6. **Transitive** *Should have been audited* includes *been* as a helper and the past participle *audited.* Always transitive.

7. Rain has been falling gently all day.

   7. **Intransitive** *Has been falling* is the verb phrase. No object.

Troublesome Verbs

Lie and *lay*, *sit* and *set*, and *rise* and *raise* are frequently misused. In each of these troublesome pairs, one verb is transitive and the other is intransitive. You should have little difficulty with them if you know their principal parts and can identify a transitive and an intransitive verb. First, review the principal parts of each pair.

PRESENT	PAST	PAST PARTICIPLE	PRESENT PARTICIPLE
lie	lay	lain	lying
lay	laid	laid	laying
sit	sat	sat	sitting
set	set	set	setting
rise	rose	risen	rising
raise	raised	raised	raising

The first verb in each of the pairs is the intransitive verb; the second is the transitive. Note that in the first verb of each pair—*lie, sit, rise*—the root form contains an *i* as its second letter. This *i* will help you remember that it is the *in*transitive form. The second verb in each of the pairs—*lay, set, raise* —is the transitive form.

Note also that *lay,* present tense, is transitive; it always has an object. But *lay,* the past tense of *lie,* is intransitive; it never has an object.

> Miss Korpi *laid* her coat on the chair. *Laid,* the transitive verb, is needed because it has an object, *coat.*
>
> The jacket *has been lying* there all morning. *Lying,* the intransitive verb, is needed because there is no object.
>
> Plans *were laid* for a major reorganization. A past participle used with a being verb, *were,* is transitive; therefore, the transitive verb *laid* is the correct choice.
>
> Both men and women *will rise* for the occasion. The intransitive verb *rise* is correct because there is no object.

✐ Practice

Select the correct verbs in the following sentences, and indicate whether each verb is transitive or intransitive.

1. I (lay, laid) on the cot in acute pain.

   1. lay   Intransitive.

2. Please (sit, set) the calendar on my desk.

   2. set   Transitive.

3. Willie (lay, laid) the necklaces carefully on the counter.

   3. laid   Transitive.

4. Our city (lies, lays) on the east side of the state.

   4. lies   Intransitive.

5. Paper (lay, laid) on the floor around the wastebasket.

   5. lay   Intransitive.

6. The porter has (sat, set) the packages on the bench.

6. **set** Transitive.

7. Who was (lying, laying) on the cot in the afternoon?

7. **lying** Intransitive.

✦ Assignment

Check your knowledge of being verbs and transitive and intransitive verbs by doing Self-Check 3; then use the Self-Check Key to evaluate your work. In addition, complete Review Sheet 3, and turn it in to your instructor for scoring.

Nouns–Part 1

YOUR OBJECTIVE
To identify nouns and add plural endings correctly.

REMEMBER . . .
The framework of the written and spoken word is the sentence.

All words within the framework are parts of speech.

Verbs, which you studied in Unit 3, are one of the parts of speech; nouns are another.

What Nouns Are

You may remember from former study of English that nouns are words that name persons, places, or things. In addition, you may remember that nouns are identified as *common* or *proper*. If a noun names a *particular* person, place, or thing, it is called a *proper* noun. All other nouns are classed as *common* nouns.

COMMON NOUNS	boy (person)	office (place)	typewriter (thing)
PROPER NOUNS	Nick Brown (*particular* person)	New York (*particular* place)	Department of Purchases (*particular* thing)

The capitalization of proper nouns will be treated in more detail in Unit 22.

Nouns may be *singular* (indicating *one* person, place, or thing) or *plural* (indicating more than one). Note the following examples:

SINGULAR	boy	office	typewriter
PLURAL	boys	offices	typewriters

⬡ Practice

Find the nouns in the following sentences; then identify them as common or proper and as singular or plural.

1. Maria Ramiro enjoys speaking to audiences.

2. An important managerial trait is efficiency.

3. Both plants will move to Michigan next year.

4. Each day make a list of the important jobs to be done.

5. Her partners will support Joe in the campaign.

1. **Maria Ramiro** Proper, singular.
   audiences Common, plural.
2. **trait** Common, singular.
   efficiency Common, singular.
3. **plants** Common, plural.
   Michigan Proper, singular.
   year Common, singular.
4. **day** Common, singular.
   list Common, singular.
   jobs Common, plural.
5. **partners** Common, plural.
   Joe Proper, singular.
   campaign Common, singular.

Spelling of Plural Nouns

The correct spelling of English plural nouns is difficult only because there is more than one way of forming them. Of course, the most common way to form a plural is to add an *s* to the singular form, as in *position* (singular), *positions* (plural). But *industry* becomes *industries*, *veto* becomes *vetoes*, and *man* becomes *men*.

The purposes of this unit are to present guides to help you spell plural forms and to alert you to the need for checking in a dictionary when special situations arise.

Plurals Formed With *ES*

Singular nouns ending in *ch, sh, s, x,* and *z* form their plurals by adding *es*. As you study the following words that illustrate this principle, notice that when you pronounce the plural forms of the words the *es* can be heard as an extra syllable.

church	churches	gas	gases	box	boxes
match	matches	address	addresses	tax	taxes
bush	bushes	glass	glasses	chintz	chintzes

The plurals of most proper names follow the same principles; that is, most proper names form their plurals by adding an *s*. But if they end in *ch, sh, s, x,* or *z*, then an *es* is added. Study the following examples and note the extra sound when the *es* is added.

Abbott	Abbotts	Kinch	Kinches	Mannix	Mannixes
Smith	Smiths	Nash	Nashes	Hernandez	Hernandezes
Berkholt	Berkholts	Flores	Floreses	Gomez	Gomezes
McCarthy	McCarthys	Jones	Joneses	Schultz	Schultzes

Titles With Names

The plural of *Mr.* is *Messrs.*, which is the abbreviation of *Messieurs* (the French word for *Misters*). *Mesdames*, a French word, is the plural of *Mrs.* The plural of *Miss* is *Misses*. *Ms.* is an abbreviation used by those who prefer a title that does not indicate marital status; its plural is *Mses.* or *Mss.* When a title is used with a name, either the title or the name may be made plural. Study the following examples:

SINGULAR	PLURAL
Mr. Lane	the *Messrs.* Lane *or* the Mr. *Lanes*
Mrs. Hill	the *Mmes.* Hill *or* the *Mesdames* Hill *or* the Mrs. *Hills*
Miss Hart	the *Misses* Hart *or* the Miss *Harts*
Ms. Marti	the *Mses.* (*or Mss.*) Marti *or* the Ms. *Martis*
Dr. Davis	the *Doctors* Davis *or* the Doctor *Davises*

🖊 Practice

Find each of the plural nouns in the following sentences, and correct those that are not properly written.

1. The Misses Johnsons have opened a new boutique.

   1. Misses Johnson *or* Miss Johnsons

2. Are the Foxs buying a ranch-style home?

   2. Foxes

3. All the bushs are sprayed with insecticides.

   3. bushes
   insecticides   Correct.

4. The John Cortezs invited all employees to visit their new stores.

   4. Cortezes
   employees   Correct.
   stores   Correct.

5. Have the two Mrs. Finch's decided to become partners?

   5. Mesdames (*or* Mmes.) Finch
   or Mrs. Finches
   partners   Correct.

Plurals of Nouns Ending in Y

When a singular noun ends in *y* preceded by a vowel—*a, e, i, o, u*—the plural is formed in the regular way, by adding an *s*. However, if the final *y* is preceded by a consonant—any letter of the alphabet other than *a, e, i, o, u*—

the plural is formed by changing the *y* to *i* and adding *es*. The following examples will help you to learn and remember this frequently needed spelling rule.

1. Final *y* preceded by a vowel — add *s*.

attorney	attorneys	valley	valleys
boy	boys	journey	journeys
key	keys	relay	relays

2. Final *y* preceded by a consonant — change *y* to *i* and add *es*.

supply	supplies	facility	facilities
community	communities	enemy	enemies
difficulty	difficulties	battery	batteries

Note: Proper names that end in *y* form their plurals by adding *s*. For example, *the two Harrys, the Averys, the Henleys*. Exceptions to this rule are the proper nouns *Alleghenies, Rockies,* and *Smokies*.

Plurals of Nouns Ending in *O*

The plural of a singular noun ending in *o* preceded by a vowel is usually formed by adding *s*. Some singular nouns ending in *o* preceded by a consonant form their plurals by adding *es*; others, by adding *s*. Study the following examples, but remember that you should consult the dictionary when you are in doubt.

1. Final *o* preceded by a vowel — add *s*.

ratio	ratios	rodeo	rodeos
patio	patios	radio	radios
studio	studios	trio	trios

2. Final *o* preceded by a consonant — add *es*.

veto	vetoes	hero	heroes
echo	echoes	torpedo	torpedoes
cargo	cargoes *or* cargos	tomato	tomatoes

3. Final *o* preceded by a consonant — add *s*.

zero	zeros *or* zeroes	piano	pianos
auto	autos	photo	photos
memo	memos	solo	solos

Plurals of Nouns Ending in *F* or *FE*

Some singular nouns ending in *f* or *fe* change the *f* or *fe* to *v* and add *es*. Others simply add *s*. At the top of the next page are some of the frequently used nouns that illustrate these endings. If you are in doubt about other nouns ending in *f* or *fe*, consult your dictionary.

half	halves	belief	beliefs
life	lives	chief	chiefs
thief	thieves	safe	safes
leaf	leaves	proof	proofs
shelf	shelves	brief	briefs
wife	wives	tariff	tariffs
wharf	wharves	dwarf	dwarfs
	or wharfs		*or* dwarves

◈ Practice

From each pair of words in parentheses choose the word that is spelled correctly.

1. Several (industrys, industries) are including closed circuit television (studios, studioes) in their plants.

    1. industries, studios

2. In the jargon of the theater (turkeys, turkies) are plays that have flopped.

    2. turkeys

3. Return the picture (proofs, prooves) by Thursday.

    3. proofs

4. New (facilitys, facilities) will improve production.

    4. facilities

5. Three (sopranos, sopranoes) each sang (solos, soloes).

    5. sopranos, solos

Vowel Changes

Some nouns form their plurals by changing one or more vowels instead of by adding *s* or *es*. A few plurals end in *en*.

VOWEL CHANGE		EN ENDING	
man	men	child	children
woman	women	ox	oxen
foot	feet		
tooth	teeth		
mouse	mice		

Apostrophe to Form Plurals

For the sake of clarity, use an apostrophe plus *s* in forming the plurals of uncapitalized letters and uncapitalized abbreviations with internal periods.

crossing the *t*'s   paying for all c.o.d.'s

Capital letters and abbreviations ending with capital letters form their plurals by adding *s* alone, as do numbers expressed in figures. In addition, words used as words are often pluralized merely by adding *s* or *es*.

ABCs	M.D.s	the pros and cons
the three *Rs*	the 1970s	no *ands*, *ifs*, or *buts*

The apostrophe is also used to show possession or the omission of letters. These uses will be studied in Units 5 and 21.

Plurals of Compound Nouns

A compound noun is a noun consisting of two or more words. When a compound noun is written as one word, pluralize the final element in the compound as if it stood alone.

drugstore	drugstores
stepchild	stepchildren
footstep	footsteps
cupful	cupfuls

An exception to this rule is the compound noun *passerby;* its plural is *passersby.*

When the parts of a compound noun are written as separate words or are joined by hyphens, pluralize the most important word in the compound.

editor in chief	editors in chief
mother-in-law	mothers-in-law
senator-elect	senators-elect
runner-up	runners-up

When a hyphenated compound does not contain a noun as one of its parts, simply pluralize the final element.

go-between	go-betweens
hand-me-down	hand-me-downs

Some compounds have two recognized plural forms. (The first plural shown below is the preferred form.)

attorney general	attorneys general, attorney generals
court-martial	courts-martial, court-martials
notary public	notaries public, notary publics

Nouns That Do Not Change Form

Some nouns have the same form both in the singular and in the plural.

deer	corps
sheep	series
moose	vermin
Japanese	salmon

Some nouns are always singular. For such nouns, use a singular verb.

honesty	Their *honesty* in business *was* well known.
news	The *news is* good.
mathematics	*Mathematics is* a required subject in school.
music	*Music evokes* many emotional responses.

Some nouns are always plural and require a plural verb.

savings	Her *savings were* depleted rapidly.
scissors	*Are* the *scissors* sharp?
trousers	His *trousers are* being mended.
credentials	The ambassador's *credentials were* approved.
proceeds	The *proceeds* from the fire sale *are* $7,500.

Nouns of Foreign Origin

Nouns of foreign origin form plurals in different ways. A few have two plural forms; use the first form listed in your dictionary, unless the meaning of each is different, as in the plurals for *index* and *medium* below. If you are in doubt, consult your dictionary. (Here and throughout, spelling is based on *Websters New Collegiate Dictionary*, G. & C. Merriam Co., Inc., Springfield, Massachusetts, 1976.)

The words illustrated below are commonly used in business.

SINGULAR	PLURAL
addendum	addenda
alumna (feminine)	alumnae
alumnus (masculine)	alumni
analysis	analyses
basis	bases
crisis	crises
criterion	criteria
datum	data
formula	formulas
index	indices (math symbols)
	indexes (of books)
medium	media (advertising and communications)
	mediums
memorandum	memorandums
parenthesis	parentheses
stimulus	stimuli

Note: The noun *data*, though plural in form, is usually followed by a singular verb in informal usage.

Their sales data *is* consistently accurate.

✐ Practice

From each pair of words in parentheses, select the correct word.

1. Messrs. Alexander and McDermott became (president-elects, presidents-elect) during the (1960's, 1960s).

    1. presidents-elect, 1960s

2. Who were the (runner-ups, runners-up)?

    2. runners-up

3. Use four (tablespoonsful, tablespoonfuls) of coffee for this percolator.

    3. tablespoonfuls

4. A service corps (was, were) formed in 1976. — 4. **was**
5. No sound (bases, basises) were established for selection policies. — 5. **bases**
6. Mathematics (is, are) a challenging study. — 6. **is**
7. In your opinion, (was, were) the goods satisfactory? — 7. **were**
8. The (addendums, addenda) were added to the report. — 8. **addenda**
9. Our (son-in-laws, sons-in-law) are all professional men. — 9. **sons-in-law**
10. Too many (*ands*, *and*'s) appear in the report. — 10. ***ands***

Assignment

Check your ability to identify nouns and to make their plural forms correctly by doing Self-Check 4; then use the Self-Check Key to evaluate your work. In addition, complete Review Sheet 4, and turn it in to your instructor for scoring.

5

Nouns–Part 2

YOUR OBJECTIVE

To use apostrophes correctly to show ownership.

REMEMBER . . .

A noun is the part of speech that names a person, place, or thing.

A noun may be singular or plural.

The plural form of most nouns is formed by adding s *or* es, *but some plurals are formed in an irregular way.*

Words Can Show Ownership

Words that show ownership are said to be in the possessive case. Both nouns and pronouns may "possess" or show ownership, but they do so in different ways. Nouns indicate ownership by the use of an apostrophe. Many pronouns change their form in the possessive. The main reason for studying possessives is to learn the correct use of the apostrophe.

Identifying Possessives

A possessive noun or pronoun is usually followed by a word that represents what it "owns." Study these examples:

> The *typist's* chair . . . .
> *Today's* paper . . . .
> *Our* report . . . .

You can identify the possessives by changing the possessive to a phrase: "the chair belonging to the typist," "the paper of today," "report belonging to us." By substituting an *of* phrase, a *by* phrase, or a phrase with *belonging to*, you can tell whether or not the possessive should be used and whether or not the possessive word ends in *s*. If you can tell whether a noun ends with an *s*, you will be able to handle apostrophes correctly in possessive forms.

Did you notice in the examples given that the nouns showed possession through the use of the apostrophe but that the pronoun *us* changed its form altogether? *Our* is the possessive form; no apostrophe is used. You will find a more detailed study of possessive pronouns at the end of this unit.

Basic Possessive Forms

Possession is normally shown by adding an apostrophe plus *s* at the end of a singular noun; for example, *yesterday's news, a month's vacation, an editor's notation, the secretary's notebook*. The rule that governs this most frequent use of the apostrophe consists of two parts:

1. When a noun *does not* end in *s*, add an apostrophe plus *s* to form the possessive. To be sure that the noun does not end in *s*, change the possessive to a phrase as suggested in the previous paragraphs.

   The *department's* goal was to increase production. Say "the goal of the department." *Department* does not end in *s*; therefore, add an apostrophe plus *s*.

   Our *company's* products are distributed widely. Say "the products of our company." *Company* does not end in *s*; therefore, add an apostrophe plus *s*.

   Roberto's car will carry all the passengers. Say "the car belonging to Roberto." *Roberto* does not end in *s*; therefore, add an apostrophe plus *s*.

   Women's dresses are on sale. *Women*, though a plural form, does not end in *s*; therefore, an apostrophe and *s* are added.

2. When a noun *does* end in *s*, add only an apostrophe to form the possessive.

   Our *employees'* cafeteria is on the fourth floor. Say "the cafeteria of the employees." *Employees* ends in *s*; therefore, only an apostrophe is added.

Two *ladies'* coats were stolen. Say "two coats belonging to ladies." *Ladies* ends in *s;* therefore, only an apostrophe is added.

Many authorities agree on two exceptions to these basic apostrophe rules:

1. An apostrophe plus *s* is added to a noun ending in *s* if an extra syllable — a *ses* sound — is heard when pronouncing the possessive.

   Mr. Jones's house is located nearby. Do you hear the extra *ses* sound when you pronounce *Jones's?*

   The *witness's* testimony will be heard today. The extra *ses* sound you hear when you pronounce *witness's* gives you the clue for adding the *apostrophe* plus *s.* If there were more than one witness, the sentence would read: **Two *witnesses'* testimony will be heard today.** Remember the spelling rule for nouns ending in *s.*

2. A modern trend is to omit the apostrophe in names of organizations and institutions except when the name ends in *men;* for example, *Lions Club, State Teachers College,* but *Businessmen's Club, Professional Women's Association.*

🖐 Practice

In each of the following sentences, apply the principles and suggestions concerning the use of the apostrophe; then select the correct word from those given in parentheses.

1. (Men's, Mens') suits and (boy's, boys') shirts are on sale.

   1. Men's, boys' Suits belonging to *men;* shirts belonging to *boys.*

2. Several (accountant's, accountants') offices opened near here.

   2. accountants' Offices of several *accountants.*

3. The (trio's, trios') latest record was a hit.

   3. trio's Latest record of the *trio.*

4. Linda (Hastings's, Hastings') resignation was accepted with regret.

   4. Hastings' The resignation of Linda *Hastings.*

5. Two (months', month's) sick leave is allowed for each employee.

   5. months' Sick leave of two *months.*

6. The (Korpinskis', Korpinski's) request will be filled.

   6. Korpinskis' The request of the *Korpinskis.*

7. (Claudius', Claudius's) vacation starts next week.

   7. Claudius's The vacation of *Claudius.* Do you hear the extra *ses* sound when the possessive is added?

8. The (painter's, painters') brush was dripping onto the carpet.

   8. painter's The brush of the painter.

Possessives of Compounds

The possessive of a compound word is formed on the *last word* of the compound. For placement of the apostrophe with this last word, follow the rules you have just learned.

Her *sister-in-law's* work record is unexcelled. *Law* is the last word in the compound and does not end in *s*.

Miss Jansen attended the *personnel directors'* conference. *Conference of personnel directors.* The last word in the compound, *directors*, does end in *s*.

The *president-elect's* campaign was *someone else's* job. *The campaign of the president-elect; job of someone else.*

Joint or Separate Ownership

Joint ownership is shown by making the last word in the combination possessive.

Juanita and Sue's locker is located near the lounge. *Juanita and Sue* share a locker; therefore, the apostrophe is used only with *Sue*, the last word in the combination.

The *secretary and the treasurer's* report was submitted promptly. The *secretary* and the *treasurer* made one report.

Separate ownership is shown by placing the apostrophe with each member of the combination. Note how the preceding sentences have been changed to show separate ownership.

Juanita's and Sue's lockers are located near the lounge. Each woman has a locker of her own. Note that the plurals *lockers* and *are* are required.

The *secretary's and the treasurer's* reports were submitted promptly. The *secretary's report* and the *treasurer's report* are now separate.

Possessives Before Gerunds

Do you remember what a *gerund* is? A *gerund* is a verb form that ends in *ing* and that is used as a noun. For example: *Working gives satisfaction; Ellen dislikes proofreading her work.* The words *working* and *proofreading* are gerunds. A noun or pronoun that immediately precedes a gerund must be in the possessive case.

The *clerk's* arriving early was a surprise to everyone. *Arriving* is a gerund; therefore, the possessive *clerk's* precedes it.

You can depend on *Mr. Baker's* doing a capable job. The possessive *Mr. Baker's* is used before the gerund *doing*.

Her winning the sales contest came as no surprise. *Winning* is a gerund; the possessive pronoun *her* precedes it.

✍ Practice

In each of the following sentences, select the correct possessive form and give a reason for your selection.

1. The (editor's in chief, editor in chief's) telephone was out of order.

1. editor in chief's The possessive is formed on the last word of a compound.

2. Are (employees' and executives', employees and executives') cafeterias on the same floor?

2. **employees' and executives'** Separate ownership; two cafeterias.

3. When will the (auditors and accountants', auditors' and accountants') meeting be held?

3. **auditors and accountants'** *One* meeting for both the *auditors* and the *accountants*.

4. Were you expecting the (mayor, mayor's) campaigning to be successful?

4. **mayor's** Possessive needed before the gerund *campaigning*.

5. (Black and Harris's, Blacks' and Harris') sponsoring of the (drum corp's, drum corps') entertainment met with instant approval.

5. **Black and Harris's** Do you hear the extra syllable *ses* in *Harris's?*
drum corps' The entertainment of the *drum corps.*

Possessives of Personal Pronouns

Personal pronouns form their possessives by changes in form rather than by the use of apostrophes. For instance, *I* becomes *my* or *mine, we* becomes *our* or *ours,* and *she* becomes *her* or *hers.* You will have no trouble writing possessive pronouns if you remember that pronouns *never* use an apostrophe to indicate possession.

My **desk has been refinished.** *My* is a possessive pronoun. No apostrophe.

Our **outlines are ready and those notes are** *ours. Our* and *ours* are possessive pronouns. No apostrophe.

Her **book is selling well, and the profit will be** *hers. Her* and *hers* are possessive pronouns. No apostrophe.

Some possessive personal pronoun forms are frequently misused because they sound like other words that have entirely different meanings (called *homonyms*). The most frequently confused are the following:

Its. This is a possessive personal pronoun meaning *belonging to it.* Many people confuse this word with *it's,* a contraction of *it is* or *it has.* If you understand that the apostrophe is *never* used with pronouns to show possession, you should have no difficulty using the possessive personal pronoun *its* and the contraction *it's.*

It's **time for careful self-evaluation.** *It is* time.

A poorly planned report soon shows *its* **weaknesses.** *Weaknesses* of *it,* the report.

Their. The three words *their, they're,* and *there* have the same sound. *Their* is a possessive pronoun meaning *belonging to them. They're* is a contraction of *they are. There* means *in that place* or *to that place.*

Their **itinerary will take them** *there* **within a week.** *Their* is a possessive pronoun (no apostrophe); *There* means *to that place.*

They're **traveling alone.** *They're* is a contraction of *they are.*

Your. Although *your* and *you're* sound alike, their meanings are different. *Your* is a possessive pronoun (no apostrophe); *you're* is a contraction of *you are.*

Your improvement in English usage shows that *you're* studying and learning. *Your* is a possessive pronoun (no apostrophe); *you're* is a contraction of *you are*.

Whose. *Whose* and *who's* also sound alike. *Whose* is a possessive pronoun meaning *belonging to whom*; *who's* is the contraction of *who is*.

The man *whose* application was neatly completed is the one *who's* being hired. *Whose*, meaning *of whom; who's*, meaning *who is*.

◉ Practice

Select the correct form in each of the following sentences.

1. (They're, Their, There) ready for a committee report.

2. (Your, You're) vacation is scheduled for July.

3. The tree spread (its, it's) shade over the lawn.

4. (Who's, Whose) carbon is this? It was lying (they're, their, there) on the floor.

5. Does she know that the job will be (your's, yours)?

6. (Its, It's) time for a rest period, but (whose, who's) ready?

7. How soon will the house be (hers, her's)?

1. **They're** Meaning *they are.*

2. **Your** Meaning *belonging to you.*

3. **its** Meaning *belonging to it.*

4. **Whose** Meaning *belonging to whom.*
there Meaning *in that place.*

5. **yours** Meaning *belonging to you.*

6. **It's** Meaning *it is.*
who's Meaning *who is.*

7. **hers** Possessive pronoun—no apostrophe.

⚏ Assignment

Check your ability to use apostrophes correctly to show possession by doing Self-Check 5; then use the Self-Check Key to evaluate your work. In addition, complete Review Sheet 5, and turn it in to your instructor for scoring.

Pronouns–Part 1

YOUR OBJECTIVE
To use the correct forms of pronouns in all sentences.

REMEMBER ...
Pronouns are words that refer to or that are used in place of nouns.

Nouns use apostrophes to show possession; pronouns do not.

Function of Pronouns

Nouns and pronouns are divided according to their function into three groups called *cases*—the nominative, the objective, and the possessive. When you studied nouns and pronouns in the possessive case, you learned that nouns use an apostrophe to show possession while pronouns change their form. Since nouns in the nominative and objective cases remain the same, they cause no special problems and need no special study. Unlike nouns, pronouns do need special study, for they change their form in each case.

The first step in studying pronoun usage is to review the nominative, the objective, and the possessive forms of the pronouns listed below.

NOMINATIVE	I	you	he	she	it	we	they	who
OBJECTIVE	me	you	him	her	it	us	them	whom
POSSESSIVE	my- mine	your- yours	his	her- hers	its	our- ours	their- theirs	whose

The rules presented here for using the nominative and objective cases are considerably simplified. However, your conscientious study and practice of them, both in and out of class, will result in mastery of pronoun usage.

Subject of Verbs

In Unit 1 you learned how to identify the subject of a sentence. Now add to that knowledge the fact that subjects are always in the nominative case.

I **typed one copy.** *I* is the subject. The nominative form is always used as the subject of a verb.

He **left early.** *He,* not *him,* is the subject of *left* and is nominative.

Who **did the filing?** The nominative *who,* rather than the objective *whom,* is correct because *who* is the subject of the verb *did.*

Predicate Nominatives

A predicate nominative is a noun or pronoun that completes the meaning of a *being* verb. You remember from your study in Unit 3 that *being* verbs (*be, am, is, are, was, were, been*) may be used in a sentence either as helper verbs or as main verbs. As helpers, *being* verbs are followed by present or past participle forms of other verbs.

> You *were talking* to Mr. Beck.
> The copy *was typed* in triplicate.

When a *being* verb is used as a main verb, it may be followed by a noun or pronoun that completes its meaning. When this happens, the noun or pronoun that follows the *being* verb must be in the nominative case.

> It was *she* who called last Wednesday morning. The nominative *she* is used following a *being* verb.
> We agreed that it is *they* who will be responsible. The nominative form *they* follows the *being* verb *is*.

𝌆 Practice

Select the correct word from those in parentheses in each of the following sentences, using the principles you have learned for pronouns in the nominative case.

1. (They, Them) are leaving now for lunch.

2. If you were (he, him), would you resign?

3. Did the caller say (who, whom) he was?

4. Mary answered the telephone by saying, "It is (I, me)."

5. It was (we, us) who sponsored the dance.

6. (Who, Whom) worked overtime?

1. **They** Subject of the verb phrase *are leaving*.

2. **he** Predicate nominative completing being verb *were*.

3. **who** Predicate nominative completing being verb *was*.

4. **I** Predicate nominative completing being verb *is*.

5. **we** Predicate nominative completing being verb *was*.

6. **Who** Subject of verb *worked*.

Objects of Verbs

In Unit 3 the object of a verb was defined as the result or the receiver of the action of a transitive verb. Whenever a pronoun is the object of a verb, that pronoun must always be in the objective case.

> The results of the poll surprised *him*. *Him*, not *he*, is the receiver of the action of the verb *surprised* and is in the objective case.
> They sent the *books* three weeks after we ordered *them*. The noun *books* is the object of the verb *sent*; the pronoun *them* is the object of the verb *ordered*. Both objects, *books* and *them*, are in the objective case.

Objects of Prepositions

Nouns and pronouns are also used as objects of such prepositions as *of, to, for, from, by, in,* and *under;* pronouns that are objects of prepositions are always in the objective case. The combination of a preposition and its object is known as a prepositional phrase. (You will study more about prepositions in Unit 12.)

> The entire staff paid tribute to *them. Them* is the object of the preposition *to* and is therefore in the objective case.
>
> Jack arranged a going-away party for *her. Her* is the object of the preposition *for.*

Subjects and Objects of Infinitives

Infinitives—basic verb forms preceded by *to*—may have both subjects and objects, just as other verb forms may. Except with *to be,* pronouns used as either subjects or objects of infinitives are in the objective case.

> They wanted *him* to translate the manual into French. *Him* is the subject of the infinitive *to translate* and is in the objective case.
>
> Cook Products Inc. asked *us* to supply *them* with three panel trucks. *Us* is the subject of the infinitive *to supply; them* is the object. Both pronouns are correctly in the objective case.

Pronouns After *To Be*

The case of a pronoun that follows *to be* depends on whether the infinitive has a subject. If *to be*—or any other infinitive—has a subject, a pronoun that follows the infinitive must be in the objective case. However, if *to be* does not have a subject, a pronoun following the infinitive must be in the nominative case.

> Mr. Burt believed the culprits to be *them. Culprits,* the subject of *to be,* is in the objective case; therefore, the predicate pronoun following *to be* is the objective, *them.*
>
> The new manager was thought to be *I. To be* has no subject in this sentence; therefore, the nominative *I* is correct to agree with the nominative case subject of the sentence, *manager.*

✒ Practice

Select the correct pronoun form, keeping in mind the basic rules for the use of the nominative and objective cases and the special rules for pronouns with infinitives.

1. Mr. Jameson lent (they, them) enough to start a business.

   1. **them** Object of a verb.

2. (Who, Whom) should we select as our temporary secretary?

   2. **Whom** Object of the verb phrase *should select.*

3. The director thought the best person to be (he, him).

   3. **him** *To be* has a subject, *person.*

4. Don't sell anything until you get an order from (I, me).

4. **me** Object of preposition *from.*

5. Miss Goode is often taken to be (she, her).

5. **she** The infinitive does not have a subject.

6. Mr. Mallory has requested (I, me) to call (they, them) twice a week to obtain the latest information.

6. **me** Subject of an infinitive. **them** Object of an infinitive.

Pronouns in Compounds

Many major errors in the use of pronouns are made when the pronoun is part of a compound subject or a compound object.

> **Give the letters to *Jean and me.*** Compound object of verb *give: give to Jean, give to me.* Requires objective case.
>
> ***Mr. Zielinski and he*** **will finish the work.** Compound subject of verb phrase *will finish. Mr. Zielinski will finish, he will finish.* Requires nominative case.

You will be able to use the correct pronoun in compounds like the preceding examples if you mentally omit everything in the compound except the pronoun. The correct form will then come to you naturally.

> **Martin and (we, us) will compute new rates.** Omit *Martin and,* and you will say: *We will compute new rates.*
>
> **The president asked Mrs. Allen and (I, me) to work overtime.** Omit *Mrs. Allen and,* and you will say: *The president asked me . . . .*
>
> **Please return the prints to (he, him) or (I, me).** Omit one of the pronouns and you will say: *Please return the prints to him,* or *Please return the prints to me.*

Case of Appositives

An *appositive* is a word or a group of words used to identify or to give additional information about a preceding noun or pronoun.

> **Mr. Egbert,** *a well-known author,* **will visit us today.** *A well-known author* gives additional information about *Mr. Egbert* and is called an appositive. Note that a comma is correctly placed before and after the words used as an appositive.

When the appositive is a noun, no problem exists, but errors in case are sometimes made when pronouns are used. To help you know which case of pronoun to use, remember that an appositive is in the same case as the word with which it is in apposition.

> **The accountants, Marcella and (he, him), are competent workers.** The pronoun is in apposition with *accountants;* its case will therefore be the same as *accountants. Accountants* is the subject of the verb *are; he,* the nominative pronoun, is correct.
>
> **Ms. Watts seldom criticizes her assistants, Mabel and (he, him).** The pronoun is in apposition with *assistants,* the object of the verb *criticizes;* therefore, the objective-case pronoun *him* is the correct pronoun.
>
> **It was the assistants, Frank and (she, her), who organized the filing system.** The pronoun is again in apposition with *assistants.* However, in this sentence *assistants* is a predicate nominative completing the meaning of the *being* verb *was;* therefore, *she* is correct.

You can speed the selection of the correct case of a pronoun in apposition by mentally omitting the word or words with which it is in apposition. The correct form will stand out immediately. Try this idea in the sentences given in the previous examples. In the first sentence, omit *the accountants* and you will say: *Marcella and he are competent workers.*

When a pronoun is used in a restrictive appositive—*we three, us workers, you men*—the correct form can be selected by mentally omitting the noun and using just the pronoun. Note that no commas are used to set off the restrictive appositive.

(We, Us) employees would like electric typewriters. Mentally omit *employees* and you will say: *We would like* .... Therefore, *we employees* is correct.

They asked (we, us) women to organize the convention. Mentally omit *women* and you will say: They asked us to organize .... Therefore, *us women* is correct.

✺ Practice

Select the correct pronouns in the following sentences. Remember to omit the extra words in the compounds and appositives to help make your selection easier.

1. The victory belongs to (he, him) and (I, me).

   1. him, me Compound objects of preposition *to.*

2. Two part-time workers, Carolyn and (she, her), helped us with the arithmetic.

   2. she Appositive of *workers,* the subject of a verb.

3. (We, Us) editors have worked hard all day.

   3. We Restrictive appositive as subject.

4. Please call Sandra and (I, me) when you are ready.

   4. me Compound object of verb *call.*

5. Mrs. Berkin asked (we, us) clerks, Willa and (I, me), to work next Saturday.

   5. us Restrictive appositive as object of verb.
      me Part of compound in apposition with *us clerks.*

6. The new employees are the first two applicants, Mr. Smith and (he, him).

   6. he In apposition with *applicants,* a predicate nominative.

≋ Assignment

Check your ability to use pronouns correctly in the nominative and objective cases by doing Self-Check 6; then use the Self-Check Key to evaluate your work. In addition, complete Review Sheet 6, and turn it in to your instructor for scoring.

Pronouns–Part 2

YOUR OBJECTIVE
To use pronouns correctly when they end in self or when they complete a clause; also, to make correct choices between who *and* whom.

REMEMBER . . .
Pronouns are words that refer to or are used in place of nouns.

Pronouns may be in the nominative, objective, or possessive case, according to their function within the sentence.

Pronouns change their form according to their function in the sentence.

Pronouns may be subjects of verbs, predicate nominatives, objects of verbs or of prepositions, or subjects or objects of infinitives.

Case of Pronouns After *Than* or *As*

When a pronoun follows *than* or *as* in an incomplete clause as part of a statement of comparison, you can determine the correct form by mentally completing the clause.

Barbara has worked here longer than (he, him). If you complete this sentence, you will say: *Barbara has worked here longer than he has worked here.* The correct answer is *he*, the subject of the understood verb *has* worked.

My son is as tall as (I, me). Completing the sentence, you would say, *My son is as tall as I am tall. I* is the correct word.

The symphony selections pleased Mr. DeSantio as much as (I, me). Supply the words to complete the meaning of the sentence. You would say: *The symphony selections pleased Mr. DeSantio as much as the selections pleased me. Me* is the correct word.

Often the difference in the case of a pronoun will change the meaning of a sentence completely. It is important when writing to be sure of your intended meaning before choosing the case of a pronoun. If you are not careful, the result may be confusing or even the direct opposite of what you meant to say.

Miss Edwards has a better opinion of Judy than *I*. Because *I* is nominative, it will be understood as the subject of the clause *than I have*.

Miss Edwards has a better opinion of Judy than *me*. Because *me* is in the objective case, it will be understood as the object of the preposition *of*. The sentence means *Miss Edwards has a better opinion of Judy than (she has of) me*.

⚙ Practice

Select the correct words to complete the following sentences. Mentally supply the words needed to complete the meaning of each sentence. If two choices are possible, explain both.

1. You can add a column of figures faster than (he, him).

2. Miss Orth liked him as much as (I, me).

3. As an employer, Mr. Martin is as understanding as (he, him).

4. He trusted the accountants as much as (they, them).

1. **he** Subject of the understood verb phrase *can add*.

2. *me* Object of the verb *liked*. (*Or* **I** Subject of the understood clause *as much as I liked him*.)

3. **he** Subject of the understood verb *is*.

4. **them** Object of the understood verb *trusted — as much as he trusted them*. (*Or* **they** Subject of the understood clause *as they did*.)

Self-Ending Pronouns

Pronouns that end in *self* or *selves* are used in two ways: (1) to add emphasis and (2) to reflect a noun or pronoun already expressed in the sentence. The singular *self*-ending pronouns are *myself, yourself, himself, herself,* and *itself. Ourselves, yourselves,* and *themselves* are the plural forms.

> **Miss Ricardo** *herself* **asked me to call Mr. Mertz.** Do you see how *herself* adds emphasis to the statement?
>
> **I** *myself* **will type the report.** Sometimes the *self*-ending pronoun appears at the end of the sentence: *I will type the report myself.* However, note that more emphasis is expressed if the *self*-ending pronoun immediately follows the word it reinforces.
>
> **Marty convinced** *himself* **not to worry.** *Himself*, the object of the verb *convinced*, reflects back to the subject of the sentence, *Marty*.
>
> **The officials evaluated** *themselves* **critically.** *Themselves*, the object, reflects back to the subject, *officials*.

Self is added only to the pronouns *my, your, him, her,* and *it; selves* is added only to *our, your, and them.* Never use *hisself* or *theirselves.* They are both incorrect.

In the two uses of *self*-ending pronouns described above, you will notice that these pronouns always refer to other nouns or pronouns in the sentence. The nouns or pronouns to which the *self*-ending forms refer are called *antecedents.* Sometimes *self*-ending pronouns are incorrectly used, as in the sentence *Are you inviting Tim and myself? Myself* is incorrect because it has no antecedent in the sentence. The sentence should be *Are you inviting Tim and me?* If you know the two uses of *self*-ending pronouns and remember that they always must refer to nouns or pronouns in the sentence, you will not use them incorrectly in place of the regular nominative and objective forms.

⚓ Practice

Select the correct pronoun in the following sentences.

1. Would you like Dorothy and (myself, I, me) to prepare the conference room?

2. Some people are able to laugh at (themselves, they, them).

3. Neither Fran nor (myself, I, me) can return before five o'clock.

4. The supervisor asked Mrs. Roth and (myself, me, I) to attend the seminar.

5. The president (himself, he, him) issued the order.

1. **me** Subject of infinitive *to leave;* pronoun has no antecedent.

2. **themselves** Object of preposition *at;* antecedent, *people.*

3. **I** Subject of verb phrase *can return.*

4. **me** Subject of infinitive; pronoun has no stated antecedent.

5. **himself** Restrictive appositive used for emphasis.

Who and *Whom* in Questions

Who-whoever and *whom-whomever* are frequently misused pronouns. You learned in Unit 6 that *who* is the nominative form and that *whom* is the objective form. Just as with other pronouns, the nominative forms *who* and *whoever* are used as the subjects of verbs, as predicate nominatives, and as the complements of *to be* when *to be* has no subject. The objective forms *whom* and *whomever* are used in the same way as other objective pronouns—as objects of verbs and prepositions and as subjects or objects of infinitives.

Who and *whom* are frequently used to introduce questions. Since questions are almost always in inverted order, remember to change a question to normal word order before deciding which pronoun to use.

> **(Who, Whom) is the woman with the new coat?** The sentence changed to normal word order would read: *The woman with the new coat is (who, whom). Who* is correct because it is the predicate nominative.

> **(Who, Whom) shall I expect at the luncheon?** Normal order: *I shall expect (who, whom) at the luncheon. Whom* is correct because it is the object of the verb phrase *shall expect.*

> **(Who, Whom) is he supposed to be?** *He is supposed to be (who, whom). Who* is correct because it follows the infinitive *to be,* which does not have its own subject.

Some *who, whom* questions are not in inverted order. This will be obvious if you cannot change the order of the words. For example:

> **(Who, Whom) will deliver these copies to Miss Grossett?** You cannot change the order of the words. *Who* is correct because it is the subject of the verb phrase *will deliver.*

> **(Whoever, Whomever) would believe such an excuse?** The order of the words cannot be changed. *Whoever* is correct because it is the subject of the verb phrase *would believe.*

To double-check yourself on the proper selection of *who* or *whom,* mentally substitute *he* or *she* for *who* and substitute *him* or *her* for *whom* after you have changed the sentence to normal word order.

(Who, Whom) should I ask? Normal order: *I should ask (who, whom)*. Substitute *he* or *him* for *who* or *whom: I should ask him. Him,* the objective form, is correct; therefore, *whom* is the correct choice.

(Who, Whom) is best qualified for the job? The sentence is in normal order. Substitute *she* or *her* for *who* or *whom: She is best qualified for the job. She,* the nominative form, is correct; therefore, *who* is the correct choice.

✿ Practice

Choose the correct word in the following sentences, and give the reason for your choice.

1. (Who, Whom) did you say was ready?

2. (Who, Whom) asked for a raise?

3. (Who, Whom) will you nominate?

4. (Who, Whom) did Ms. Protic ask to work overtime?

5. (Who, Whom) will Mr. Shulman send to New York?

1. **Who** *You did say who (he) was ready.* Subject of verb *was.*

2. **Who** Not inverted. Subject of verb *asked.*

3. **Whom** *You will nominate whom (him).* Object of verb phrase *will nominate.*

4. **Whom** *Ms. Protic will ask whom (him) to work overtime.* Subject of infinitive *to work.*

5. **Whom** *Mr. Shulman will send whom (him) to New York.* Object of verb phrase *will send.*

Who and Whom in Clauses

Who-whoever and *whom-whomever* do not always come at the beginning of questions, as they did in the preceding discussion. Many times they are used to introduce clauses within a sentence. In order to practice separating a clause from the rest of the sentence, review the following principle. To isolate a *who* or *whom* clause within a sentence, start with *who-whoever* or *whom-whomever* and see which words following it seem to "go together."

> **No one knows (who, whom) the winner will be.** Isolate the clause *(who, whom) the winner will be.*
>
> **His best friend is a man (who, whom) everyone admires.** Isolate the clause *(who, whom) everyone admires.*
>
> **Be courteous to (whoever, whomever) calls on the telephone.** The clause is *(whoever, whomever) calls on the telephone.*
>
> **Clare, (who, whom) is very friendly, talks to everyone.** The clause is *(who, whom) is very friendly.*

After you have learned to isolate the clause, the next step is to put the clause into normal order if it is inverted, just as you did in your study of *who* or *whom* questions. If the clause needs a *subject* or a *predicate nominative,* you will select *who* or *whoever;* if it needs an *object of a verb, of a preposi-*

tion, or *of an infinitive,* you will select *whom* or *whomever.* Finally, double-check your choice of pronoun by substituting *he* or *she* for *who-whoever* and *him* or *her* for *whom-whomever.* Study the clauses isolated in the preceding examples:

> **(Who, Whom) the winner will be.** Change the clause to normal order: *the winner will be (who, whom). Who* is correct, predicate nominative following a *being* verb. Note that you could also substitute *he.*
>
> **(Who, Whom) everyone admires.** Change the order to normal: *everyone admires whom. Whom* is correct, object of the verb *admires.*
>
> **(Whoever, Whomever) calls on the telephone.** This clause is in normal order. Note that you cannot change it. The correct choice is *whoever,* subject of verb *calls.*
>
> **(Who, Whom) is very friendly.** This clause is in normal order. The correct choice is *who,* subject of the verb *is.*

Practice

In the following sentences, (1) isolate the who *or* whom *clauses; (2) change any inverted clauses to normal order; (3) select the correct pronoun; and (4) give the reason for your choice.*

1. Bob Bruno, (who, whom) you met last week, will be the sales manager.

   1. **whom** *You met whom (him) last week. Whom* is object of verb *met.*

2. We will consider (whoever, whomever) applies to be our representative.

   2. **whoever** *Whoever (he) applies to be our representative.* Subject of verb *applies.*

3. Do you know (who, whom) they will select?

   3. **whom** *They will select whom (him). Whom* is object of verb *will select.*

4. Mr. Kelso did not say (who, whom) will help with the campaign.

   4. **who** *Who (he) will help with the campaign.* Subject of verb phrase *will help.*

5. Mr. Kelso did not say (who, whom) he has selected to plan the campaign.

   5. **whom** *He has selected whom (him).* Object of verb phrase *has selected.*

6. Joyce is the person (who, whom) will need least supervision.

   6. **who** *Who (he) will need least supervision.* Subject of verb phrase *will need.*

Assignment

Check your ability to use pronouns correctly when they complete a clause or when they end in self, *and check your ability to make correct choices between* who *and* whom *by doing Self-Check 7; then use the Self-Check Key to evaluate your work. In addition, complete Review Sheet 7, and turn it in to your instructor for scoring.*

 # Subject-Verb Agreement

YOUR OBJECTIVE
To use singular verbs with singular subjects, plural verbs with plural subjects.

REMEMBER...
A *simple subject shows* who is speaking, who is spoken to, *or* the person or thing spoken about.

A *simple predicate shows the action of the subject or expresses a condition or state of being.*

Basic Agreement Principle

The basic agreement principle is this: A singular subject requires a singular verb, and a plural subject requires a plural verb. This principle applies to all sentences and clauses except the "condition contrary to fact" clauses discussed later in this unit.

A *meter is* slightly longer than a yard. The simple subject is *meter,* a singular noun; the verb *is* is correct.

This *artist paints* both city and rural scenes. The simple subject is *artist,* a singular noun; the verb *paints* is also singular.

The *folders,* all clearly marked, *were presented* at the meeting. The simple subject is *folders,* a plural noun; the verb phrase *were presented* is also plural.

One of our benefits *is* insurance protection. The simple subject is *one,* which is singular; the singular verb is *is. (Benefits* is object of the preposition *of.)*

You have learned that most *nouns* change from singular to plural by adding *s* or *es;* for example, *day—days, boy—boys, box—boxes.* Notice that in the sample sentence above, the verb *paints* agrees with the singular noun *artist.* This is because in the present tense a *verb* adds an *s* or *es* to agree with singular nouns and the singular pronouns *he, she,* and *it.*

Study the agreement of nouns and pronouns with their predicate verbs given below. Note that the pronoun *you* may refer to one person or more than one but that *you* is always used with a plural verb form.

SINGULAR NOUNS	PLURAL NOUNS	SINGULAR PRONOUNS	PLURAL PRONOUNS
Tom knows	the Haleys know	I know	we know
the city knows	the cities know	you know	you know
the office knows	the offices know	he, she, it knows	they know

Because mistakes in agreement often occur with the irregular helping verbs, be sure to study the present and past tense forms of *have* and *be* listed below. Note again that *you* used as a singular or a plural is always followed by the plural verb form.

SINGULAR		PLURAL	
I am/was	I have/had	we are/were	we have/had
you are/were	you have/had	you are/were	you have/had
he, she, it is/was	he, she, it has/had	they are/were	they have/had

🖋 Practice

Identify the simple subject; then select the verb that correctly agrees with it. To help identify the subject, remember to change the sentence to normal order if it is written in inverted order.

1. One of you (is, are) hiding the truth.

    1. One *is*

2. Next to Mr. Baker (is, are) seated the principal speaker.

    2. speaker *is* seated

3. The candidates who are vigorously campaigning (have, has) written their own speeches.

    3. candidates *have* written

4. The key to the file cabinets (is, are) on my key ring.

    4. key *is.*

5. Here (come, comes) two of my best friends.

    5. two *come*

6. Several renters who live at that address (pay, pays) rent on an annual basis.

    6. renters *pay*

Compound Subjects Joined by *And*

So far in your study of agreement you have been concerned with one-word subjects, but you will recall that the subject of a sentence may also be a compound. It is particularly important that you learn to use the correct verb form when the subject of a sentence is a compound joined by *and, or,* or *nor.*

A compound subject made up of two or more equally important words joined by *and* requires a plural verb.

> The *original and* the *copy have* been filed. *Original and copy* is a compound made up of singular nouns joined by *and.* The verb that agrees with the compound is *have been filed.*
>
> *Miss Davis and Mr. Benson work* well as a team. The two names joined by *and* form a compound subject that requires the plural verb *work.*

Selecting the correct verb in sentences like these is normally not a difficult problem. However, there are two instances in which a compound with *and* takes a singular verb; mistakes are commonly made in these cases. Please study carefully the two exceptions to the rule about compounds joined by *and.*

1. When the parts of a compound subject joined by *and* denote the same person or thing, a singular verb is required.

A famous *author and lecturer is* scheduled to speak at the conference. In this case, the two words *author* and *lecturer* refer to one person. Therefore, a singular verb is needed.

Ham and eggs is a favorite American breakfast. Here *ham and eggs* is considered as one unit; therefore, it is correctly followed by a singular verb.

2. When a compound subject joined by *and* is preceded by *each, every, many an,* or *many a,* a singular verb is used.

Every typewriter, calculator, and duplicator *was* needed to complete this report on time. The singular verb *was* is correct because the elements of the compound subject are joined by *and* and the subject is preceded by *every*.

Many a man and woman *has* complimented our executive training program. The singular verb *has complimented* is correct because the compound subject is preceded by *many a*.

Practice

Select the correct verb to complete the following sentences, which have compound subjects joined by and. *Remember the exceptions to the basic rule of agreement.*

1. Accuracy and speed (is, are) important in typewriting.

   1. are

2. Mr. Trent and his assistant (try, tries) to remain available for sales calls.

   2. try

3. Every business and industry (expect, expects) to earn a profit.

   3. expects

4. The manager and comptroller (expect, expects) to move from her present office.

   4. expects   One person.

5. Several men and women (expect, expects) to receive a bonus this year.

   5. expect

6. Both the workers and the work (is, are) well organized.

   6. are

Compound Subjects Joined by *Or* or *Nor*

When a compound subject is joined by *or* or *nor*, the verb agrees with the part of the compound nearer (or nearest) the verb.

John *or* Sam *plans* to stay until five o'clock. The singular verb *plans* agrees with *Sam*, the noun nearer the verb.

Neither Elsie *nor* the *stenographers are* prepared for this latest rush project. The plural verb *are prepared* agrees with *stenographers*, the noun closer to the verb.

Either Donna *or Dave is* assigned to receive the special training. The verb *is assigned* agrees with the singular noun *Dave*, which immediately precedes it.

✎ Practice

In the following sentences, select the correct verb to agree with the compound subjects joined by or *or* nor.

1. Neither Mr. Jackson, his secretary, nor I (is, are, am) responsible for the production schedule.

   1. **am** This verb agrees with *I*, the part of the compound subject nearest it.

2. The offset machine or the liquid duplicators (is, are) in first-class operating condition.

   2. **are** Agrees with *duplicators.*

3. Either the typewriter or the copy machine (is, are) in need of repair.

   3. **is** Agrees with *machine.*

4. Neither Joan nor Marge (take, takes) advantage of the reference library.

   4. **takes** Agrees with *Marge.*

5. Neither Mrs. Baker nor her helpers (take, takes) advantage of the reference library.

   5. **take** Agrees with *helpers.*

There at Beginning of Sentence or Clause

Many sentences and clauses begin with *there* followed directly by a verb — *there is, there have been,* etc. In these sentences or clauses, the subject *follows* the verb. To find the subject, change the sentence from inverted order to normal order.

> There (is, are) many letter forms illustrated in this book. Normal order: *Many letter forms are illustrated in this book.* The correct verb is *are.*
>
> Everyone believed that there (was, were) a mistake in Mr. Jason's report. *A mistake was in Mr. Jason's report.* The correct verb is *was.*

✎ Practice

Select the correct verb for each sentence below. Remember to invert the sentences or clauses beginning with there *to find the subject.*

1. We learned that there (was, were) three men planning the latest project.

   1. **were** *Men* is plural.

2. There (have, has) been too many filing errors in this section.

   2. **have** *Errors* is plural.

3. There (is, are) enough copies for everyone to see.

   3. **are** *Copies* is plural.

4. (Was, Were) there eight or ten reams in the package?

   4. **Were** *Reams* is plural.

5. There (is, are) a sales agent and two job applicants in the reception lounge.

   5. **are** Agrees with a compound subject joined by *and.*

If, As If, As Though, Wish

In some instances it is correct to use *were* in sentences where ordinarily you would use *was*. Use *were* after the verb *wish* and after the words *if, as if,* and *as though* when those words express a condition that is not true or that is highly doubtful.

Ann *wishes* she *were* on vacation. But she is not.

If I *were* you, I would accept. But you cannot be someone else.

She acts *as if* she *were* the president of the company. But she is not.

I act *as though* I *were* the boss. But I am not.

Mr. Donet looked *as though* he *was* ill. He may have been ill; therefore, the verb *was* is used after *as though* in this sentence.

If Jack *was* at the airport (and he was), I did not see him. *If* introduces a true statement; thus *was* is correct.

Practice

Select the correct verb for each of the following sentences.

1. I wish Bert (was, were) working with us.

    1. **were** After *wish.*

2. If it (was, were) not for the accuracy of the secretaries, our costs would soar.

    2. **was** After *if* in true statement.

3. She acted as if she (was, were) the Queen of England.

    3. **were** After *as if,* contrary to fact.

4. If Sara (was, were) in your position, she would be angry.

    4. **were** After *if,* contrary to fact.

5. It seemed as though the type bar (was, were) out of line.

    5. **was** *As though* introduces a statement that may be true; it is *not* highly doubtful.

Assignment

Check your ability to make subjects and predicates agree by doing Self-Check 8; then use the Self-Check Key to evaluate your work. In addition, complete Review Sheet 8, and turn it in to your instructor for scoring.

Pronoun-Antecedent Agreement

YOUR OBJECTIVE
To use pronouns that agree with their antecedents.

REMEMBER...
A pronoun is a word that refers to or takes the place of a noun or another pronoun.

Nouns and pronouns, according to their function, may be in the nominative, objective, or possessive case.

An antecedent is the noun or other pronoun for which a pronoun stands.

Agreement of Pronouns With Antecedents

A pronoun must agree with its antecedent in number, gender, and person. If its antecedent is singular, the pronoun must be singular; if its antecedent is plural, the pronoun must be plural.

A pronoun and its antecedent also must agree in gender—masculine, feminine, or neuter. However, agreement in gender is of concern only in connection with the use of third person singular pronouns (*she, her, hers; he, him, his; it, its*); these are the only pronouns that reflect gender.

Finally, a pronoun must agree with its antecedent in person—first, second, or third. A first person pronoun is one that refers to the speaker (*I, me, my, mine, we, us, our,* or *ours*). A second person pronoun (*you, your,* or *yours*) refers to the person spoken to. A third person pronoun (*he, she, they, their,* or *him,* for example) refers to the person or thing spoken about. All nouns are considered to be third person.

I paid *my* bill on time. The antecedent of *my* is *I.* Both pronouns are singular; both are of common gender (either masculine or feminine); and both are first person.

Miss Brooks paid *her* bill on time. The antecedent of *her* is *Miss Brooks.* Both are third person, singular, and feminine.

Mr. Brown paid *his* bill on time. The antecedent of *his* is *Mr. Brown.* Both are third person, singular, and masculine.

Some antecedents, such as *student* and *employee,* may be either masculine or feminine.

Apparently the student misplaced *his* identification card. In this case, the student is a man.

The new employee should complete *her* insurance form before she leaves the personnel department. The employee is a woman.

When such common-gender nouns refer generally to *any* student or employee, use a pronoun form such as *he or she* or *him or her* to refer to the noun.

> A student who misplaces *his or her* identification card should report the loss immediately.

> A new employee should complete *his or her* insurance form before *he or she* leaves the personnel department.

The rules for subject-verb agreement that were discussed in Unit 8 will help you to determine whether a singular or a plural pronoun is needed. For example, if the antecedent of a pronoun consists of two nouns of equal importance joined by *and*, the compound is considered a plural both for verb agreement and for pronoun reference.

> *Mary and Beth have* finished *their* reports. *Mary and Beth*, the compound subject and antecedent of the pronoun, requires the plural pronoun form *their* and the plural verb form *have*.

✷ Practice

Choose the word or words that correctly complete each sentence below. Remember that pronouns must agree with their antecedents and that verbs must agree with their subjects.

1. Our receptionist found the coat and a sample case and took (it, them) to the office.

   1. **them** Plural; antecedent is compound subject joined by *and*.

2. Profits from passenger service (is, are) expected to remain at (its, their) present level.

   2. **are, their** The subject of the verb and the antecedent of the pronoun is the plural noun *profits*.

3. A sales agent using these new methods will be able to increase (his, his or her, their) contacts by 50 percent.

   3. **his or her** Agrees with *agent*, a singular noun referring to either a man or a woman.

4. Either Mrs. Benson or her daughter had been managing the accounts (herself, themselves).

   4. **herself** The antecedent is a compound joined by *or* and is singular.

5. People who like clothes (is, are) usually conscious of (his, his or her, their) appearance.

   5. **are, their** *People* is plural.

Indefinite Words

The indefinite words *each, either, neither, everyone, everybody, someone, somebody, anyone, nobody, no one, a person* are always singular in meaning and are always in the third person. Therefore, pronouns referring to these indefinite words will be singular and third person (*he, she, he or she, it*).

Everyone *has* to report *his or her* (not *your*) absence. *Has* and *his or her* agree with the singular subject *everyone.*

Neither of the department heads *is* willing to relinquish *her* office. *Neither* is the subject and is always considered singular; therefore, *is* and *her* are correct.

🖊 Practice

Select the correct word to complete each sentence.

1. Each navigator and flight attendant (was, were) responsible for (his or her, their) own duties.

   1. **was, his or her** The compound subject is preceded by *each,* making it singular; the gender of *navigator* and *flight attendant* is unspecified.

2. Anybody interested in continuing (your, his or her, their) education is eligible for the Learn-As-You-Earn program.

   2. **his or her** *Anybody* is singular; the gender is unspecified.

3. Everyone who visited the exhibits (was, were) given a souvenir to take with (him, him or her, them).

   3. **was, him or her.** To agree with *everyone.*

4. Either of the women will arrange (her, their) time to suit the revised schedule.

   4. **her** *Her* agrees in number with *either; her* agrees with *women* only in gender.

Collective Nouns

A *collective noun* is one whose singular form refers to a group of persons or a collection of things; for example, *committee, company, audience,* or *council.* In most cases a collective noun requires singular verbs and pronouns because it is considered a single, whole unit. Occasionally, however, a collective noun that is singular in form is used in a way that suggests individuals acting separately and is therefore correctly treated as a plural noun—that is, the verbs and pronouns that refer to the collective noun are plural forms. Since using plural verbs and plural pronouns with a noun that is singular in form may result in an awkward-sounding sentence, it is generally better to rephrase the sentence.

The audience *has* shown *its* approval of the performance. *Audience,* a collective noun, is used to suggest action as a single unit; *has* and *its,* singular forms, are correct.

The committee *were* arguing among *themselves.* The collective noun *committee* is used to suggest individuals acting separately; therefore, the use of the plural forms *were* and *themselves* is correct. The sentence would be less awkward if it were rephrased: *The members of the committee were arguing among themselves.*

Agreement With Nouns of Foreign Origin

In Unit 4 you learned that some nouns borrowed from foreign languages have irregular plural forms. For example, some singular nouns ending in *um—*

datum, addendum — have plurals ending in *a* — *data, addenda*. Other singular nouns ending in *is* — *crisis, basis* — have *es* plural endings — *crises, bases*.

You have to know whether a foreign noun is singular or plural in order to make verbs and pronouns agree with it in number. If you are in doubt about the singular or plural form of a foreign noun, consult a dictionary.

> The alumnae *have* been asked to give *their* support. *Have* and *their* are correct because *alumnae* is plural.

> Mr. Poe sees the basis for your opinion, but he thinks *it* is incorrect. Because *basis* is singular, *it* is the correct pronoun.

✐ Practice

Select the correct pronouns (and verbs or nouns where necessary) referring to collective and foreign nouns.

1. Type the parentheses in (its, their) proper (place, places).

2. Have you read about the crises? Do you understand (its, their) implications?

3. The group (was, were) practicing (its, their) Christmas program.

4. The public expressed (its, their) views on education.

5. We studied the economic analyses but were not sure how to report (it, them).

1. **their, places** *Parentheses* is plural.

2. **their** *Crises* is the plural of *crisis*.

3. **was, its** *Group* is a collective noun considered as a unit.

4. **its** If *public* is considered a group.
   their If considered as individuals acting separately.

5. **them** *Analyses* is plural.

Agreement in Relative Clauses

As you know, a clause contains a subject and a verb but, unlike a sentence, does not in itself express a complete thought. A *relative clause* is a clause introduced by a relative pronoun. Agreement of pronouns and of verbs in relative clauses is sometimes a problem, but if you are aware of the following four principles, you will be able to handle subject-verb agreement and pronoun-antecedent agreement within relative clauses.

1. The relative pronouns are *who, whose, whom* — used for persons; *which* — used for things; and *that* — used for either persons or things.
2. These pronouns are called *relative* because they *relate* the clause to its antecedent — the word to which the clause refers.
3. The antecedent is usually — but not always — the noun or pronoun occurring immediately before the relative pronoun.
4. Verbs and pronouns in relative clauses agree in person and number with the antecedent of the relative pronoun.

> Martha is an *expert who is* always expected to perform her work accurately. Do you see that *who* is a relative pronoun? It relates the clause it introduces to its antecedent, *expert*.

These are *problems that have* no easy solution. *That* is a relative pronoun. Its antecedent is *problems,* which is plural and requires the plural verb *have.*

This is our new filing *system, which is* being used on a trial basis. *Which* is a relative pronoun; its antecedent is *system,* which is singular and requires a singular verb.

John is one of those *men who resist* change in *their* daily routine. *Who* is a relative pronoun; the antecedent is *men.* Therefore, the plural forms *resist* and *their* are correctly used.

You will discover that it is *I who am* afraid. The antecedent of *who* is *I,* which is correctly followed by *am.* Note the *that* in this example is not a relative pronoun because it has no antecedent.

She is a *supervisor whom* we all respect and *whose* ideas are appreciated. The antecedent of both *whom* and *whose* is *supervisor. Whom,* not *who,* is required because in normal order the clause reads *we all respect whom.*

Practice

Before you select the correct words in the following sentences, identify the relative pronoun. Can you find the antecedent? Do you know that the verb in a relative clause agrees with the antecedent of the relative pronoun?

1. Ellen is one of those women who (make, makes) friends wherever (he, she, they) (go, goes).
2. Did you purchase one of the new dishwashers that (is, are) fully automatic?
3. You will soon see the flowers and plaque that (is, are) to honor the company's first anniversary.
4. It is I who (is, are, am) in need of assistance.
5. What does management think of the committee that (make, makes) (his, its, their) suggestions for company improvements?

1. **make, they, go** Agree with antecedent *women.*
2. **are** Agrees with *dishwashers.*
3. **are** Agrees with compound antecedent *flowers and plaque.*
4. **am** Agrees with *I.*
5. **makes, its** Agree with *committee,* a collective noun.

Assignment

Check your ability to use pronouns that agree with their antecedents by doing Self-Check 9; then use the Self-Check Key to evaluate your work. In addition, complete Review Sheet 9, and turn it in to your instructor for scoring.

Adjectives

YOUR OBJECTIVE
To use adjectives correctly so that you can create clear, descriptive sentences.

REMEMBER ...
Overworked adjectives, such as terrific, good, awful, *can be replaced with others that are more expressive.*

Nouns are words that name persons, places, or things.

Words are classified according to their function within the sentence.

Recognizing Adjectives

Adjectives are words that describe or modify nouns. If they describe, they are picture-making words, such as *attractive* display, *purple* dress, *happy* people. If they tell *how much* or *how many*, they are modifying words, such as *large* package, *several* folders, *three* days, *second* door, *last* page. Some words may act as nouns in one sentence or as verbs or adjectives in others. To discover the classification of any word, therefore, check its use in a particular sentence.

The *contract* is already signed. *Contract* in this sentence is a noun used as the simple subject.

The Smith Company will *contract* for the management service. Here *contract* is a verb, part of the verb phrase *will contract*, used as the simple predicate.

Contract negotiations are continuing throughout the year. Here *contract* is an adjective describing the noun *negotiations*.

𝕊 Practice

Select the adjectives in the following sentences, then find the nouns that they modify or describe.

1. Can you find the red and green pencils used for final proofreading of the annual report?

1. **red, green** Describe *pencils*.
   final Describes *proofreading*.
   annual Describes *report*.

2. The weary old woman slumped into the nearest vacant seat in the reception area.

2. weary, old   Describe *woman.*
   nearest, vacant   Describe *seat.*
   reception   Describes *area.*

3. Two copies of the insurance report will be filed with the new representative.

3. **Two**   Modifies *copies.*
   insurance   Describes *report.*
   new   Describes *representative.*

Note: The articles *a, an,* and *the* are sometimes called adjectives, but it is more convenient for our purposes to think of articles as a separate type of word.

Comparison of Adjectives

Adjectives can show differences in degree of the qualities they express. For example, one person is *healthy,* a second may be *healthier,* and a third may be the *healthiest.* Do you see that the changes in the forms of the adjectives reflect changes in the degree of healthiness? There are three degrees of comparison that may show *more* or *less* of a given quality:

Positive. Used when the word the adjective describes is not compared with anything else.

Your office is *large.*

Comparative. Used to express a higher or lower degree when *two* things are being compared.

Your office is *larger* than mine. *Larger* expresses a higher degree.
My office is *smaller* than yours. *Smaller* expresses a lower degree.

Superlative. Used to denote the highest or lowest degree when *three or more* things are being compared.

Your office is the *largest* one on the floor.

Adjectives are compared in the following three ways:

1. The endings *er* for the comparative and *est* for the superlative degree are added to most one-syllable words and to some two-syllable words.

POSITIVE	COMPARATIVE	SUPERLATIVE
fast	faster	fastest
firm	firmer	firmest
simple	simpler	simplest

2. *More* and *most* are used with the positive forms of most adjectives of two or more syllables to form the comparative and superlative degrees.

POSITIVE	COMPARATIVE	SUPERLATIVE
capable	more capable	most capable
common	more common	most common
efficient	more efficient	most efficient

Less and *least*, which are comparative and superlative forms that show decreasing degree, also precede positive forms.

POSITIVE	COMPARATIVE	SUPERLATIVE
reliable	less reliable	least reliable
common	less common	least common
expensive	less expensive	least expensive

Note: Some two-syllable adjectives can be compared by adding *er* and *est* endings or by using *more* and *most:*

lovely—lovelier, loveliest	*or*	more lovely, most lovely
sorry—sorrier, sorriest	*or*	more sorry, most sorry

3. Some adjectives change their forms completely for the comparative and superlative degrees.

POSITIVE	COMPARATIVE	SUPERLATIVE
good	better	best
much, many	more	most
bad, ill	worse	worst
little	less *or* littler	least *or* littlest

A common adjective-usage error—double comparison—occurs when two forms of comparison are used at the same time.

Mr. Mills is *taller* than Mr. Jones. Not *more taller*.

Choice of Comparative or Superlative Degree

When comparing two persons, places, or things, use the comparative degree. When comparing three or more persons, places, or things, use the superlative degree.

Both copy machines are good, but the *newer* one is *better*. *Both* signifies *two;* therefore, the comparative degree must be used.

All the desks are neat, but Martha's is the *neatest*. *All* means *more than two;* therefore, the superlative form is correct.

Harold is the *older* of the two men, but Sam is the *oldest* person in his department. *Older,* the comparative form, is correctly used for comparing *two* persons; *oldest,* the superlative, is correct for comparing *more than two* persons.

🖋 Practice

Select the correct word in each of the following sentences. Be sure to avoid double comparisons. Give the reason for your selection.

1. This desk is the (higher, more higher, highest) of the two.

2. Martha is (lonelier, more lonelier) now that Sue has left.

1. higher   Comparative degree used for comparison of two desks. *More higher* would be a double comparison.

2. lonelier   *More lonelier* would be a double comparison.

3. Which person on your staff is the (most reliable, reliablest)?

3. **most reliable**   Three-syllable words form the superlative by using *most*.

4. Jane must soon decide which is the (better, best) job for her, records clerk or data clerk.

4. **better**   Referring to *two* jobs.

5. James must soon decide which is the (better, best) job for him—records clerk, coding clerk, or data clerk.

5. **best**   Referring to *more than two* jobs.

Other, Else, and All in Comparisons

When a person or thing is compared with the group to which it belongs, the word *other* or *else* is used in expressing the comparative degree.

> This furniture is less expensive than any *other* I can find. If the word *other* were not used, the sentence would indicate that this furniture is less expensive than itself.

> You will find more books in the new library than in any *other* library in the state. Without the word *other*, the sentence would suggest that the new library is not in the state and that it has more books than itself.

> Mr. Valdez's **report** is more detailed than anyone *else's*. If the word *else's* is omitted, the sentence would compare *report* with *anyone*. Of course, the report must be compared with another *report*.

With the superlative degree, the word *all* is used. Do not use *any*. For example:

> Pat is the most industrious of *all* our employees.

Adjectives That Cannot Be Compared

There are some adjectives that cannot be compared. They can be used only in the positive degree because of the nature of their meaning. For instance, consider the adjective *round*. If a ball is *round*, another ball cannot be *more round*. Being *round* is an absolute condition. Some other *absolute adjectives* —those that cannot be compared—are listed below.

complete	level	straight
correct	perfect	unanimous
dead	right	unique

Sometimes there is a need to indicate the degree to which a person or thing *approaches* the full meaning of an absolute adjective. If so, *nearly, more nearly, most nearly, less nearly,* or *least nearly* may be used.

> Of the three circles that John drew, the third is *most nearly* round. Since *round* is an exact condition, it may be that none of the three drawn were actually round; one, however, would be *most nearly round*; another would be *least nearly round*.

> Mary's paper is perfect; Sue's is *nearly* perfect; Dave's is *least nearly* perfect. One paper is perfect; the others show varying degrees *approaching* perfection.

✐ Practice

The following sentences will give you practice in using comparisons requiring the words other *or* all *and in handling adjectives that cannot be compared. Select the correct word and give the reason for your choice.*

1. The third file drawer is the (emptiest, most nearly empty, most empty) one in the cabinet.

   1. **most nearly empty** *Empty* cannot be compared.

2. (No, No other) store has a better reputation than ours.

   2. **No other** *No store* would exclude "our" store.

3. Los Angeles is larger than (any, any other) city in California.

   3. **any other** It cannot be larger than itself.

4. Mrs. Drown won the election in the (most, most nearly) unanimous vote ever cast in our city.

   4. **most nearly** *Unanimous* cannot be compared.

5. Your recommendations are the clearest of (all the, any of the) ones submitted.

   5. **all the** Use *all*, not *any*, with the superlative degree.

Compound Adjectives

A *compound adjective* is made up of two or more words used as a unit to modify a noun. Such a compound is usually hyphenated when it occurs before a noun.

air-conditioned office	**middle-aged person**	**three-story building**
first-class typist	**thirty-day note**	**up-to-date machinery**

Notice that the hyphenated modifying words must be used as a unit. In *air-conditioned office,* you can see that it is not an *air* office or a *conditioned* office; both *air* and *conditioned* must be used together to give the proper meaning.

Modifying words that occur *after* the noun are hyphenated only (1) if they are normally spelled with a hyphen (such as fractions and compound numbers—*one-third, three-fourths, twenty-third, fifty-first,* etc.) and (2) if they are words to inverted order (*high-priced, tax-exempt,* etc.). Check an up-to-date dictionary if you are not sure of the spelling.

Yesterday a *well-known* author visited our bookshop. *Well-known* is hyphenated because the words come before the noun they modify and are used as a unit.

The author who visited our bookstore yesterday is *well known.* *Well known* follows the noun modified; therefore, no hyphen is used.

If the first word of a compound adjective ends in *ly,* as in *smoothly operating machine,* no hyphen is used. Further, if each adjective modifies the noun separately, use a comma to show the separation.

Our *new, well-organized* plant opened last March. *New* and *well-organized,* two adjectives modifying the noun *plant,* are separated with a comma.

Practice

Check your understanding of the correct way to write compound adjectives by making the proper selection in each of the following sentences.

1. The building is located in an (out of the way, out-of-the-way) street.

2. Were you working on the (twenty first, twenty-first) floor?

3. The supply is (one fourth, one-fourth) depleted.

4. Linda is a (highly qualified, highly-qualified) secretary.

5. Did you know that this building is (government owned, government-owned)?

1. **out-of-the-way** Words used as a unit to modify *street.*

2. **twenty-first** Words normally spelled with a hyphen.

3. **one-fourth** This modifier is always hyphenated.

4. **highly qualified** No hyphen generally used in *ly* compound.

5. **government-owned** Inverted; normally spelled with a hyphen.

Those or *Them*, *Sort* and *Kind*

The pronoun *them* is sometimes misused for the adjective *those.* Never use *them* as an adjective.

> He will take *those* documents to the meeting. Not *them documents.*
> He will take *them* to the meeting. The pronoun *them* is correct because there is no noun immediately following it.

Errors are sometimes made when *this, that, these,* and *those* are used as adjectives—especially when they modify the words *kind(s)* and *sort(s).* *This* and *that* are singular and are correctly used to modify such singular nouns as *kind* and *sort. These* and *those* are plural and are correctly used to modify such plural nouns as *kinds* and *sorts.*

> We ordered six of each of *these kinds* of ball-point pens. More than one kind is indicated; therefore, the plural adjective *these* is correctly used to modify the plural noun *kinds.*
> Do you understand *this sort* of error? Only one sort of error is indicated; therefore, *this* is correct.

Practice

Select the appropriate words in the following sentences.

1. Please evaluate (those, them) charts for Miss Rogers.

2. Which of these (kind, kinds) of stationery do you prefer?

1. **those** Never use *them* as an adjective.

2. **kinds** Follows plural modifier *these.*

3. (This, These) sort of file cabinet will be purchased in the future.

3. **This**   Singular word *sort* follows.

4. All of us agree that (them, those) proofs are of poor quality.

4. **those**   Never use *them* as an adjective.

5. Janice, have you filed (those, them) sales letters?

5. **those**   Adjective modifying *sales letters*.

✘ Assignment

Check your correct use of adjectives by doing Self-Check 10; then use the Self-Check Key to evaluate your work. In addition, complete Review Sheet 10, and turn it in to your instructor for scoring.

Adverbs

Definition of Adverbs

An adverb is a word that describes, explains, or limits a verb, an adjective, or another adverb. As you study this definition, you will see that adverbs do the same job adjectives do—but they do it for different parts of speech. Note the following similarities:

1. Adverbs, like adjectives, have three degrees: the positive, the comparative, and the superlative.

2. Adverbs, too, describe or limit the word they modify. They usually answer one of the following questions: "When?" "Where?" "How?" "Why?" "How much?" "How little?" "To what extent?"

Most adjectives can be changed to adverbs by adding *ly*. For example, *quick* is an adjective; *quickly* is an adverb. Because of this *ly* ending, most adverbs are easy to recognize. However, there are several commonly used adverbs that do not end in *ly:*

always	never	rather	together
away	now	soon	too
here	once	then	very
much	quite	there	well

Judy will return *soon*. *Soon* is an adverb modifying the verb phrase *will return*. It answers the question *When?* "Judy will return *when?*" Soon.

She can finish the letter *quickly*. *Quickly* modifies the verb phrase *can finish*. It answers the question *How?*

He is *nearly* finished with the dictation. *Nearly* modifies the verb phrase *is finished*. It answers the question *To what extent?*

You are *too* early to see the announcement. *Too* modifies the adjective *early*. It answers the question *How much?*

⚙ Practice

Can you tell whether an adverb or an adjective is needed in each of the following sentences? Remember to check by using the adverb questions.

1. Everyone listened (close, closely).

1. **closely**   How?   Modifies verb *listened.*

2. Jet planes fly (swifter, more swiftly) than propeller models.

2. **more swiftly**   How? Modifies verb *fly.*

3. Mr. Robb's son won the contest (easy, easily).

3. **easily**   How? Modifies verb *won.*

4. Do you expect (immediate, immediately) results?

4. **immediate**   Adjective needed to modify noun *results.* None of the adverb questions can be answered.

5. Yes, Miss Dent, the results were announced (immediate, immediately).

5. **immediately**   When? Modifies verb phrase *were announced.*

Adverb or Adjective After Verbs

Some speakers and writers do not know whether to use an adverb or an adjective after such verbs as *appear, sound, look, feel, taste,* and *smell.* You can make the correct choice if you remember that in some sentences these verbs are action verbs and in other sentences they are *being* verbs. (See Unit 3.) When one of these verbs can be replaced by some form of the verb *be*, it is a *being* verb and should be followed by an adjective.

> The orange *tastes sweet*. *Tastes* is a *being* verb—it can be replaced with another *being* verb, *is*, and is therefore followed by the adjective *sweet*. Note that there is no action shown by the verb *tastes*. The orange itself can't *taste* anything.
>
> The gong *sounded loud*. *Sounded* is a *being* verb and is followed by the adjective *loud*. The gong itself cannot perform an action, and *sounded* can be replaced with *was*.
>
> Robert *sounded* the gong *loudly*. Here *sounded* is an action verb and is correctly followed by the adverb *loudly*.

Remember that an action verb can be modified by an adverb; a *being* verb is followed by a predicate adjective.

🖈 Practice

Decide whether these sentences have action or being *verbs; then select the appropriate adverbs or adjectives from those shown in parentheses.*

1. Your voice sounds (clear, clearly) over the telephone.

2. He feels (bad, badly) about the mistake he made.

3. The crowd appeared (quick, quickly) when the sale was announced.

4. The crowd appeared (anxious, anxiously) about the storm warnings.

5. This perfume smells (strong, strongly).

1. **clear** *Sounds* is a *being* verb; adjective is needed.

2. **bad** *Feels* is a *being* verb; adjective is needed.

3. **quickly** *Appeared* is an action verb; adverb is needed.

4. **anxious** *Appeared* in this sentence is a *being* verb and can be replaced by *was*; adjective is needed.

5. **strong** *Smells* is a *being* verb; adjective is needed.

Adverb and Adjective Confusion

Several pairs of adjective-adverb forms are commonly misused, yet the choice of the correct form follows the same rules that have already been studied. You should have no difficulty with the words if you remember that the first word in each of the following pairs is the adjective and the second is the adverb.

> **Sure–Surely.** *Sure* is an adjective; *surely*, an adverb.
>
> Do you know of a *sure* way to promote this new product? *Sure* modifies the noun *way*; therefore, the adjective form is correct.
>
> You *surely* know which product sells best. The adverb *surely* modifies the verb *know*.

Real–Really. *Real* is an adjective; *really,* an adverb.

This artificial turf looks like *real* grass. The adjective *real* modifies the noun *grass.*

The office has a *really* efficient atmosphere. The adverb *really* modifies the adjective *efficient.*

Good–Well. *Good* is the adjective and *well* is the adverb, except when referring to health. To answer the question "How?" use *well;* otherwise, use *good.* However, when speaking of health, always use *well.*

Tom is a *good* driver. *Good* modifies the noun *driver. Good* is an adjective; it does *not* answer the question "How?"

Tom drives *well.* Drives how? *Well.*

Mary felt *well* soon after her operation. When referring to health, use *well.*

Some–Somewhat. *Some* is the adjective; *somewhat,* the adverb.

Ray is *somewhat* reluctant to see Mr. Powers. The adverb form *somewhat* modifies the adjective *reluctant.*

We need to order *some* new supplies. The adjective form *some* modifies the noun *supplies.*

Most–Almost. *Most* is an adjective, the superlative form of *much* or *many* (*many, more, most*). *Almost* is an adverb meaning *not quite* or *very nearly. Most* is *not* a shortened form of *almost.*

By noon the filing was *almost* finished. Very nearly *finished.*

Most customers see *almost* all the merchandise on the first floor. Many, more, *most customers see* very nearly *all* . . . .

💋 Practice

Select the correct words from the pairs in parentheses.

1. The true story is (real, really) shocking.

   1. **really**   Adverb modifying adjective *shocking.*

2. Marie has (most, almost) decided to type (most, almost) of the correspondence.

   2. **almost**   Very nearly *decided.*
   most   Adjective modifying *correspondence.*

3. (Some, Somewhat) typists are (some, somewhat) careless about proofreading.

   3. **Some**   Adjective modifying *typists.*
   somewhat   Adverb modifying adjective *careless.*

4. (Good, Well) secretaries perform (good, well) when they feel (good, well).

   4. **good**   Modifies *secretaries.*
   well   Answers the question "How?" Modifies verb *perform.*
   well   Refers to health.

5. Tim tells a story (real, really) (good, well).

   5. **really well**   Adverb *really* modifies adverb *well.* (*Well* modifies the verb *tells.*) Both adverbs answer question "How?"

Position of the Adverb

An adverb should be placed as close as possible to the word it modifies; otherwise, the sentence may not mean what is intended. Notice how the meaning changes in the following sentence when the adverb *only* is moved.

Only my brother painted his apartment last month. No one else painted it.
My *only* brother painted his apartment last month. I have just one brother.
My brother *only* painted his apartment last month. He did nothing else to it.
My brother painted *only* his apartment last month. He did not paint anything else.
My brother painted his *only* apartment last month. He has just one apartment.
My brother painted his apartment *only* last month. It was just last month that he painted it.

⚙ Practice

Relocate the adverb in each sentence below to make the meaning of the sentence clearer. More than one meaning may be possible.

1. The lot was sold for $500 only.

   1. . . . for only $500. What a low price! (*Or* Only the lot . . . . The building brought more. *Or* The only lot . . . . It was the last one available.)

2. We just expect to leave in one hour.

   2. . . . to leave in just one hour. No more or no less.

3. Robert ate three pieces of pie alone.

   3. Robert alone ate . . . . Robert ate the three pieces by himself, without anyone else's help.

4. Study will help you only learn the facts.

   4. Only study will help . . . . (*Or* . . . will only help you learn . . . . *Or* . . . to learn only the facts.)

Adverb Confusion

Both *never* and *not* are adverbs, and they are sometimes confused. Remember that *never* means *not ever, at no time;* it always refers to time. *Not* simply expresses negation.

We have *not* received your check. Not *We never received your check.*
Mr. Hansen did *not* ask us to verify the account. Not *Mr. Hansen never asked us . . . .*
Hadley's has *never* offered a special discount to any retail customer. *Never* is correctly used in this sentence.

Double Negatives

Scarcely, only, hardly, but, and *never* are negative in meaning. No other negative such as *not,* can correctly be used with them.

It was so foggy that Mark *could scarcely* see the edge of the road. Not *Mark could not scarcely see . . . .*

Why doesn't the manager *ever* use the front entrance? Not *Why doesn't the manager never . . . .* It is correct, however, to say, *Why does the manager never . . . .*

I *have only* one comment to make. Not *I haven't only . . . .*

🎗 Practice

Watch for the negative words in the following sentences. Avoid double negatives and the confusion of never *for* not.

1. The Dickens order (did not specify, never specified) how the merchandise was to be shipped.

2. I couldn't (help but think, help thinking) of a long walk in the country.

3. Miss Elliot (can't hardly, can hardly) help looking worried.

4. The experiment (was not authorized, was never authorized) by the president.

5. Mr. Thompson (has scarcely, hasn't scarcely) time to do his own work.

6. Do you realize that Mrs. Milton (did not close, never closed) her store before eight o'clock?

1. **did not specify** *Never* is too strong for this message.

2. **help thinking** To avoid the double negative *couldn't . . . but.*

3. **can hardly** *Can't hardly* is a double negative.

4. **was not authorized** *Never* is too strong for this message.

5. **has scarcely** *Hasn't scarcely* is a double negative.

6. **never closed** Using *never* emphasizes the fact that the store was always open until eight o'clock.

≈ Assignment

Check your ability to choose correctly the adverb or the adjective form by doing Self-Check 11; then use the Self-Check Key to evaluate your work. In addition, complete Review Sheet 11, and turn it in to your instructor for scoring.

Prepositions

YOUR OBJECTIVE
To learn about specific problems that writers and speakers have with prepositions so that you can use prepositions correctly.

REMEMBER . . .
A prepositional phrase is made up of a preposition and its object.

A pronoun that is the object of a preposition is in the objective case.

Prepositional Phrases

A preposition is a connecting word that shows the relationship between a noun or a pronoun and some other word in a sentence. The preposition and the noun or pronoun that follows, together with any modifiers, are called a *prepositional phrase.* For example:

The Senator wrote *to us* last week *about his campaign. To us* is a prepositional phrase. The preposition *to* shows the relationship between the objective case pronoun *us* and the word that the phrase modifies—*wrote. About his campaign* is also a prepositional phrase. *About* is the preposition relating *campaign* to *wrote.*

For further review, study the commonly used prepositions in the following list:

about	before	except	like	to
above	below	for	of	under
after	beside	from	on	upon
among	between	in	onto	until
at	by	into	over	with

Although prepositions are automatically used correctly in most instances, there are several points that often cause errors. Therefore, give close attention to the following rules of correct usage.

Words Requiring Specific Prepositions

Some words must be followed by specific prepositions. Because these words are frequently used in business communications, you should study them carefully.

Agree on or upon (reach an understanding), Agree With (a person), Agree to (a plan). Use *agree with* when the object of the preposition is a person.

Everyone *agreed on* the prices proposed by the sales personnel.
Everyone *agreed with* the sales personnel.
Everyone *agreed to* the proposal made by the sales personnel.

Angry With (persons), Angry at (things or conditions). Use *angry with* when the object of the preposition is a person; use *angry at* when the object is not a person.

Martha was not *angry with* me for forgetting our date.
Martha is *angry at* the necessity for working late.

Part From (a person), Part With (a thing). Use *part from* when the object of the preposition is a person; use *part with* when the object is not a person.

As long-time employees, we dislike *parting from* our retiring manager.
Tony refuses to *part with* his old car.

In Regard to, With Regard to, As Regards. Each of these three phrases is correct, and they may be used interchangeably. A common error is using *regards* rather than *regard* in *in regard to* and *with regard to*.

May we talk to Mrs. Kay *with regard* (or *in regard*) *to* our suggestion? Not *with regards* or *in regards*.
As regards personnel policies, who sets company policy?

Different From, Identical With, Retroactive to. The correct prepositions in these phrases cannot be explained in any special way; they can only be memorized to assure correct usage.

Modern equipment may be *different from* ours. Not *different than*.
Is your salary raise *retroactive to* July 1? Not *retroactive from*.
His estimate was *identical with* ours. Not *identical to*.

🖊 Practice

After reviewing the five preceding usage principles for prepositions, select the preposition that correctly completes each sentence.

1. Is the quality of this bond paper different (from, than) that of the letterhead paper?

   1. **from** *Different* is followed by *from*.

2. Ms. Darwin is angry (with, at) her assistant for delaying the steel shipment.

   2. **with** Angry *with* people.

3. May's suggestion is identical (with, to) Carolyn's.

   3. **with** *Identical* is followed by *with*.

4. Being angry (with, at) your typewriter does not improve your work.

   4. **at** Angry *at* conditions or things.

5. The effective salary increase is retroactive (to, from) May 1.

   5. **to** *Retroactive* is followed by *to*.

6. (In regard, In regards) to what subject is the upcoming meeting?

6. **In regard**   Not *regards*.

7. My daughter will not part (from, with) her favorite photographs.

7. **with**   Part *with* things; part *from* persons.

Other Words Requiring Specific Prepositions

Besides the commonly used phrases just studied, there are other words that require specific prepositions. The following list will provide an opportunity for you to study and check on your personal usage.

abide *by* a decision
abide *with* a person
adapted *to* (adjusted to)
adapted *for* (made over for)
adapted *from* a work
buy *from* (not *of*)
compliance *with*
comply *with*
confer *on* or *upon* (give to)
confer *with* (talk to)

confide *in* (place confidence in)
confide *to* (entrust to)
conform *to*
conformity *with*
convenient *for* (suitable for)
convenient *to* (nearby)
correspond *to* or *with* (match; agree with)
correspond *with* (exchange correspondence)

deal *in* goods or services
deal *with* people
employ *for* a purpose
employed *at* a certain salary or place
employed *in, on,* or *upon* a work or a business
planning or plan *to* (not *on*)
profit *by* (not *from*)
wait *for* (to expect)
wait *on* (to serve)

Practice

Refer to the preceding list if you are not certain of the correct usage in the following sentences.

1. The driver waited (for, on) us.

1. for

2. We must buy (from, of) the company that submits the lowest bid.

2. from

3. The lounge is convenient (to, for) relaxation, and it is especially convenient (to, for) the library, which is next door.

3. for, to

4. Merton and Merton deals (with, in) stocks and bonds.

4. in

5. I agree that all of us can profit (from, by) our mistakes.

5. by

Some Troublesome Prepositions

Some prepositions are commonly misused. These prepositions are confused with others that seem similar but that are actually used in different ways. Several preposition pitfalls are presented on the next page.

Between, Among. *Between* is commonly used when referring to *two* persons, places, or objects; *among*, when referring to *more than two*. Remember: Let the *tw* in *between* remind you of the *tw* in *two*.

Between *you* and *him,* the work will soon be completed.
The remaining work was divided *between* the *two stenographers.*
The remaining work was divided *among* the *three stenographers.*

Beside, Besides. *Beside* means "by the side of"; *besides* means "in addition to."

Place the chair *beside* the desk.
What chair, *besides* this one, can be used?

Inside, Outside. Do not use *of* after *inside* or *outside*. When referring to a period of time, use *within*, not *inside of*.

The receptionist's desk is just *inside* the entrance. Not *inside of.*
What is your hobby *outside* office hours? Not *outside of.*
Please pay your account *within* ten days. Not *inside of.*

All, Both. Use *of* after *all* or *both* only when *all* or *both* is followed by a *pronoun.*

All *of us* are eager to make *all the money* we can. *All of* is followed by the pronoun *us; all* precedes the noun *money.*
Both *of them* reported that *both the machines* were in need of repair. *Both of them,* but *both the machines.*

At, To; In, Into. *At* and *in* denote position. *To* and *into* signify motion.

Mr. King was *at* his desk early this morning. Can you see him sitting there *at* his desk?
Mr. King went *to* his office early this morning. Can you see him moving *toward* his office?
The lost letter was *in* the wrong tray, as I discovered when I went *into* the office. The letter was *in* a particular position. I was moving; therefore, I went *into* the office.

When either *at* or *in* refers to a place, use *in* for larger places and *at* for smaller:

Rita lives *in* Chicago and works *at* an exclusive specialty store.

Behind, In Back of. Use *behind*, not *in back of*. *In front of*, however, is correct.

Mr. Higgins likes best to work *behind* closed doors. Not *in back of.*
A plant guard stands *in front of* the gate.

From, Off. *From* is used when referring to persons; *off*, to things.

You can borrow an umbrella *from* Jenny. *From Jenny,* a person.
You may move the adding machine *off* your desk. *Off your desk,* a thing.

🔷 Practice

The following sentences will help you check your knowledge of correct preposition usage.

1. Your desk will be just (behind, in back of) the post, but in front of the window.

   1. behind

2. Were you (at, to) the counter when Mrs. Gardner came (in, into) the store last Thursday?

   2. at, into

3. The board announced that the profits would be divided (between, among) the stockholders.

   3. among

4. The receptionist's desk was moved (outside, outside of) the main office (inside, inside of, within) a short time.

   4. outside, within

5. Nobody (beside, besides) Mr. Earle would stand (beside, besides) Ben in the controversy.

   5. besides, beside

6. Take the money (from, off) the table and buy a ticket (from, off) Bob.

   6. off, from

Preposition Illiteracies

Some preposition errors are especially annoying in speech and in writing. For example:

Of, Have. Have is often part of a verb phrase following the helping verbs *could, should, might,* etc. *Of* is a preposition and is not used in a verb phrase. Writing or saying *of* for *have* is a common error, perhaps caused by mispronunciation. Instead of "should *have*," many people say "shuduf" and, incorrectly, write "should *of*."

The systems analyst *couldn't have* had sufficient help. Not *couldn't of.*
Alice *would have* replied sharply. Not *would of.*

Where . . . at, Where . . . to. It is incorrect to use either *at* or *to* after the word *where.*

Do you know where John is now? Not *Do you know where John is at now?*
Where did Mr. Raines go? Not *Where did Mr. Raines go to?*

Off, Off of, Off From. Of or *from* after the word *off* is incorrect.

Did you push the atlas *off* the shelf? Not *off of.*
Take the stapler *off* my desk. Not *off of.*
I borrowed a dollar *from* Judith. Not *off from* or *off of* Judith.

✪ Practice

See if you can avoid preposition illiteracies in the following sentences.

1. I know where the lost folder (is, is at).   1. **is**

2. Who should (of, have) been selected?   2. **have**

3. No one was strong enough to move the machine (off, off from) the table.   3. **off**

4. The metric tables might (of, have) been distributed earlier.   4. **have**

5. None of us knows where he (went, went to).   5. **went**

✖ Assignment

Check your ability to avoid preposition pitfalls by doing Self-Check 12; then use the Self-Check Key to evaluate your work. In addition, complete Review Sheet 12, and turn it in to your instructor for scoring.

Conjunctions

YOUR OBJECTIVE
To recognize the uses of coordinate, correlative, and subordinate conjunctions and to be able to use conjunctions correctly in sentences.

REMEMBER . . .
The sentence is the framework for expressing thoughts.

Each word within a sentence may be classified according to function.

Prepositions are connective words that show the relationship between a noun or pronoun and some other word in the sentence.

A clause has a verb in it; a phrase does not.

Conjunctions—Connective Words

You may remember that a conjunction connects words, phrases, or clauses and that it may be classified according to its function.

Coordinate. Words used to connect words, phrases, or clauses of *equal* grammatical value.

Correlative. Pairs of words used to connect words, phrases, or clauses of *equal* grammatical value.

Subordinate. Words used to connect clauses of *unequal* grammatical rank.

Recognizing conjunctions and the functions they serve within the sentence will help you understand correct comma usage, particularly in Unit 17.

Coordinate Conjunctions

Coordinate conjunctions connect two or more grammatically equal elements, such as two or more words, two or more phrases, or two or more clauses. Study the following list of common coordinate conjunctions.

accordingly	but	however	nevertheless	therefore
also	consequently	likewise	nor	thus
and	furthermore	moreover	or	yet

Note in the following examples that the words, phrases, or clauses connected by the conjunctions are of equal rank.

Mrs. Marchetti's son *and* daughter are working with us on a part-time basis. To connect *words*.

In the morning *and* after our coffee break, we will try the new machine. To connect *phrases*.

They were curious, *but* they did not ask questions. To connect *clauses*.

Correlative Conjunctions

Correlative conjunctions are coordinate conjunctions used in pairs. For example:

as (*or* so) . . . . as	neither . . . . . . nor
both . . . . and	not only . . . . . but also
either. . . . . or	whether . . . . . or

Like other coordinate conjunctions, correlatives connect *words, phrases,* or *clauses* of equal grammatical value.

Neither a letter *nor* a telephone call would be appropriate now. A pair of conjunctions is needed to connect the two nouns. Note that *neither* is correctly followed by *nor*, not *or*.

Mr. Tate is *not only* intelligent *but also* experienced. A pair of connectives is needed to connect two adjectives in this sentence.

Subordinate Conjunctions

Subordinate conjunctions connect clauses of *unequal* grammatical value—they connect dependent (subordinate) clauses with independent (main) clauses. Some of the common subordinate conjunctions are listed here.

after	before	in case	till	when
although	for	in order that	then	whenever
as	how	since	though	where
as if	if	so that	unless	wherever
because	inasmuch as	that	until	while

In studying the example sentences that follow, note that the subordinate conjunction connects a subordinate (or dependent) clause to the main (or independent) clause. The *main clause* is one that can stand alone to make a complete thought. The *subordinate clause* cannot stand alone—it must be connected to the main clause. You will study more about main and subordinate clauses when you study punctuation in Units 16 and 17.

> File the letters *whenever* you have time. *Whenever you have time* is a subordinate clause; *whenever* is a subordinate conjunction. (*File the letters* is an independent clause; it can stand alone.)
>
> *Since* the new bridge opened, traffic control has been improved. *Since the new bridge opened* is a subordinate clause; *since* is a subordinate conjunction. (*Traffic control has been improved* is an independent clause; it can stand alone.)

🖐 Practice

Can you recognize the different kinds of conjunctions? Identify the conjunction in each of the following sentences and classify it as coordinate, correlative, *or* subordinate.

1. If you are ready, let's go to lunch.

2. Is there a surplus, or should I order more?

3. Both Alice and her sister are dancers.

4. When Bruce is late, Henry opens the store.

5. Make all corrections not only on the original but also on the copies.

1. **If**   Subordinate.

2. **or**   Coordinate.

3. **Both . . . and**   Correlative.

4. **When**   Subordinate.

5. **not only . . . but also**   Correlative.

Parallel Construction

If two or more ideas are parallel, they should be expressed in parallel, or matching, constructions. For example, if a noun or a pronoun precedes a coordinate conjunction, a noun or a pronoun should follow the conjunction; if a modifying phrase precedes the coordinate conjunction, a similar modifying phrase should follow the conjunction; and so on. To apply the principle of parallel construction, remember that coordinate conjunctions must connect *like* elements.

Bill is honest, capable, *and* ought to be promoted. This sentence does *not* illustrate parallel construction. The coordinate conjunction *and* is preceded by two *adjectives* and followed by a *verb*.

Bill is honest, capable, **and worthy of promotion.** This sentence *does* illustrate parallel construction. The coordinate conjunction *and* is preceded by two *adjectives* and followed by an *adjective*.

I need *both* **the originals** *and* **the carbons.** Each conjunction is followed by a noun; therefore, the construction *is* parallel.

You must *either* **go to the post office** *or* **to the bank.** There is no match in this sentence because *either* is followed by a verb (*go*) and *or* is followed by a prepositional phrase.

You must go *either* **to the post office** *or* **to the bank.** The construction is now parallel because *either* is followed by a prepositional phrase and *or* is also followed by a prepositional phrase.

✍ Practice

One sentence in each of the following pairs is correct; the other, incorrect. Select the sentence that illustrates parallel construction.

1. a. The new library has both a good stock of fiction and nonfiction.
   b. The new library has a good stock of both fiction and nonfiction.

1. **b** *Both* fiction *and* nonfiction.

2. a. Try to talk neither too much nor too little.
   b. Try to neither talk too much nor too little.

2. **a** *Neither* too much *nor* too little.

3. a. You have both the personality and you have the background for that job.
   b. You have both the personality and the background for that job.

3. **b** *Both* the personality *and* the background.

4. a. Jack was undecided whether he should take the test now or to wait.
   b. Jack was undecided whether to take the test now or to wait.

4. **b** *Whether* to take . . . *or* to wait.

Some Troublesome Conjunctions

Some conjunction errors are made frequently and therefore merit special study. There is no special explanation to help you understand how to avoid them. Only careful study and memorization will help.

***And* for *But*.** Whenever two clauses express contrasting or opposing ideas, use the conjunction *but*—not *and*.

Larry is quick, *but* Clara is quicker. Not *and*.
The copy is ready to be printed, *but* Mr. Baker has not yet signed it. Not *and*.

Because, Where,* and *Like* for *That. You are correct to say *the reason is that,* not *the reason is because.* Also, you *read in the paper that* or *see by the notice that,* not *where.* You *pretend that,* not *pretend like.*

> The *reason* the accident happened *was that* the brakes failed. Not *reason was because.*
>
> Did you *see* in the paper *that* electrical appliances are on sale? Not *see where.*
>
> *Pretend that* you do not see her. Not *pretend like.*

Being That* for *Since, Because,* or *As. There is no such conjunction as *being that,* yet it is frequently misused for *since, because,* or *as.*

> *Because* we are united, we can present a firm platform. Not *Being that we are united . . . .*
>
> *As* she was close to the phone, Joanne answered it when it rang. Not *Being that she was close . . . .*

Like* for *As, As If,* or *As Though. The preposition *like* is often incorrectly used as a conjunction to introduce a clause, especially when part of the clause is unexpressed. In such sentences, careful writers would use *as, as if,* or *as though.*

> Tim worked tirelessly, *as* we knew he would. Not *like. As* introduces a clause.
>
> It looks *as though* it might rain. Not *like.*
>
> You act *as if* you are tired. Not *like.*
>
> Now, *as* in the summer, we should try to conserve water whenever possible. Not *like in the summer.* Part of the clause *as we should in the summer* has been omitted.

Practice

Review the five preceding topics. Then select the correct conjunctions for the following sentences.

1. The reason for the change in organization is (because, that) Mrs. Randolph resigned.
2. She was eager to leave, (but, and) her work was not finished.
3. You look (like, as if) you are happy.
4. Pretend (that, like) you are a new employee.
5. I saw on the bulletin board (where, that) a bowling league is being formed.

1. **that** *Reason is that,* not *because.*
2. **but** Use *but* for contrast.
3. **as if** Conjunction needed to introduce a clause.
4. **that** *Pretend that,* not *like.*
5. **that** *See* or *read that,* not *where.*

Assignment

Check your ability to recognize and use conjunctions correctly by doing Self-Check 13; then use the Self-Check Key to evaluate your work. In addition, complete Review Sheet 13, and turn it in to your instructor for scoring.

14 The Period

YOUR OBJECTIVE
To know when periods are needed and when they are not.

REMEMBER . . .
A sentence is a group of words that expresses a complete thought.

An independent clause can stand alone; a dependent clause cannot stand alone.

Prepositions and conjunctions connect words, phrases, or clauses within the sentence.

The Period

Punctuation marks are used in written communication to give signals that make the message clear to the reader. The period is the signal that indicates a full stop—a complete break in thought.

For the most part, you no doubt already handle period usage correctly; however, a brief review is presented here. Emphasis is placed on where periods are needed and on places where they are often incorrectly used.

Uses of the Period

Three uses of the period are presented in the following paragraphs. In the illustrations given for each of these situations, note that the period is used at the end of a complete thought to signal a full stop.

1. A period indicates the end of a declarative or an imperative sentence.

   Mr. Dexter went to the meeting. This is a declarative sentence, one that makes a statement.

   Please answer this correspondence promptly. This is an imperative sentence, one that expresses a command or an entreaty.

2. A period follows an indirect question—a statement about a question that has been asked.

   Mrs. Fry asked whether she could help Nancy. This states that Mrs. Fry asked something. If Mrs. Fry's actual words had been used, quotations and a question mark would follow: *Mrs. Fry asked, "May I help Nancy?"*

   The supervisor inquired whether there would be a fee for the service. Can you change this indirect question to a direct question? How would it be punctuated?

3. A period (not a question mark) follows a polite request phrased as a question. Such sentences often occur in the last paragraph of a business letter.

May we have your payment by return mail. No question is intended—the reader is expected to send a check immediately.

Will you verify the order number. Because *Verify the order number* might sound harsh, the request is phrased more politely as a question but is followed by a period.

✪ Practice

Select the correct punctuation mark from those given in parentheses. Can you tell why you make each choice?

1. Ms. Wright asked how many representatives were hired (period, question mark)

   1. **period**   Indirect question.

2. Will you please send the references Mr. Burns requested (period, question mark)

   2. **period**   Polite request, not a question.

3. Matt asked whether he is expected to work late (period, question mark)

   3. **period**   Indirect question.

4. Be sure all price quotations are correct (period, question mark)

   4. **period**   Imperative sentence.

5. Will you please check all price quotations (period, question mark)

   5. **period**   Polite request.

Period Fault

A common mistake made in period usage is placing a period after a group of words that does *not* express a complete thought. This error is called a *period fault.* To avoid this error, you must be able to distinguish a complete thought from one that is incomplete. Review Unit 1 if you have doubts about your ability to make this distinction.

> **We are submitting a check for Invoice 3146. As you requested.** Period fault. Notice that *As you requested* is not a sentence. Correctly written, the sentence would read: *We are submitting a check for Invoice 3146, as you requested.*
>
> **Cancellations are expected. Since the towels were not marked as irregulars.** Another period fault. A comma should be used in place of the period after *expected.*

Sometimes periods correctly follow groups of words that do not have subjects or verbs but do express more or less complete thoughts. Such groups of words are always closely related to sentences that immediately precede or follow them, and their unstated subjects or verbs are clearly understood.

> **We have finished the first unit.** *Now for the second.*
> *Meeting deadlines.* **This is our most important job.**

Comma Fault

Two separate complete thoughts should be written either as two separate sentences or as clauses held together in one sentence by a connective. Joining two such complete thoughts with only a comma results in the mistake known as a *comma fault*. The most effective way to correct this mistake is to replace the comma with a period.

Mr. Guilford is a systems analyst, he received his training at our local university. Do you see that there should have been a complete break in thought after *analyst?* A period should have been used to separate two complete thoughts.

Our chief editor is very much in demand as a speaker, she has had much lecturing experience. A period is needed in place of the comma. Do you see that each part of the sentence before and after the comma makes sense by itself?

Practice

Is the comma or the period the correct punctuation mark in the following sentences? Why?

1. For months we worked harmoniously (period, comma) no one was dissatisfied.

   1. **period** Two distinct thoughts —two sentences.

2. We are returning your invoice dated June 1 (period, comma) since this form is incomplete.

   2. **comma** This is one sentence. Note the connective *since.*

3. A sale on suits was advertised (period, comma) with summer weights a special feature.

   3. **comma** This is one sentence. Note the connective *with.*

4. You will find the suits fit well (period, comma) they are carefully tailored.

   4. **period** Two thoughts written with no connective word.

5. The style is a popular one (period, comma) though it is not becoming to tall women.

   5. **comma** One sentence. Note the connective *though.*

Instances Where Periods Are Not Used

The following are five specific instances in which periods are *not* used.

1. Periods are not used after any centered heading or title.

   Unit 1: The Sentence   (Chapter heading)
   Office Automation   (Centered title)

2. Periods are not used after numbers or letters *enclosed in parentheses.* For example, in the following skeleton outline:

   I.
     A.
     B.
       1.
       2.
         a.
         b.
           (1)
           (2)
             (a)
             (b)

   (Do use periods after letters and numbers alone.)

   (But do *not* use periods after letters and numbers in parentheses.)

3. Periods are generally not used after single words or short phrases in tabulated lists or in outlines.

> **The unit is divided into the following main parts:**
> 1. **When to use a period**
> 2. **When not to use a period**

However, if each item is a long phrase, a clause, or a complete sentence, a period is used.

> **These are two important points for you to remember:**
> 1. **A period brings the reader to a full stop.**
> 2. **By itself, a comma cannot join two independent clauses. A comma *and a conjunction*, however, can join two independent clauses.**

4. Only *one* period is needed to indicate a full stop at the close of a sentence ending in an abbreviation.

> **The consultant expects to arrive before 10 a.m. Not *10 a.m.*.**

5. Periods are not used as decimal points with even amounts of dollars except in tabulated, or columnar, material.

> **The price of the table is $98.60. The cost to you will be $95 if you send a check with your order. Note *$95*, not *$95.* or *$95.00.***

⚓ Practice

Indicate your choice of the correct form given in parentheses in each of the following sentences.

1. She has recently received her Ph.D. (one period, two periods)

   1. **one period** Only one mark of punctuation needed to end a sentence.

2. Cassette players costing more than ($45.00, $45) are on the third floor.

   2. **$45** No period, no zeros.

3. Two items must be considered:
   (a) When to evaluate the equipment (period, no period)
   (b) How to make the evaluation (period, no period)

   3. **no periods in (*a*) or (*b*)** No period is used after a single word or a short phrase.

4. One book cost $18.95; the other, ($30.00, $30., $30).

   4. **$30** Only the period at the end of the sentence is required.

≋ Assignment

Check your ability to use periods correctly in places where periods are needed and where they are often incorrectly used by doing Self-Check 14; then use the Self-Check Key to evaluate your work. In addition, complete Review Sheet 14, and turn it in to your instructor for scoring.

 # The Question Mark and the Exclamation Point

YOUR OBJECTIVE

To use question marks after direct questions; to use exclamation points after words or thoughts that express strong feeling.

REMEMBER . . .

A sentence is a group of words that expresses a complete thought.

Punctuation marks guide the reader to follow the thoughts expressed in writing.

The Question Mark

To the reader the question mark, like the period, indicates a full stop in thought. There are three specific instances where a question mark is used:

1. The question mark is used after a direct question.

   When will you be ready?
   What is causing the delay?

2. The question mark is used after a short, direct question that comes at the end of a statement.

   She plans to be married soon, doesn't she? This sentence begins as a statement but ends as a question. The correct end punctuation is a question mark.
   You saw the requisition, didn't you? Another question that starts as a statement.

3. The question mark is used after each item in a series of questions within the same sentence.

   Who has the most experience—Mary? Janet? Larry? The question mark correctly follows each part of the series.
   For this sentence is the correct punctuation mark a period? a comma? a question mark? Note that the separate items in the series are not capitalized.

Review of Related Rules

In the preceding unit you learned that a period, not a question mark, is the correct punctuation after (a) an indirect question and (b) a request written in the form of a question for the sake of courtesy. Study the following examples:

Where is the new restaurant located? This is a direct question, and the question mark is needed.

Milton asked where the new restaurant is located. This is an *indirect* question. It is really a statement, so the period is correct.

May I have your check by return mail. This is a polite request, practically an order. The period is therefore correct.

🌀 Practice

Indicate the correct punctuation for the following sentences. Explain your choices.

1. Mr. Vinson requested a transfer, did he not (period, question mark)

   1. **question mark** A short question following a statement.

2. Who will be in charge of the sales campaign (period, question mark)

   2. **question mark** Direct question.

3. Miss Fonda asked me if the computations would be ready by noon (period, question mark)

   3. **period** Indirect question.

4. Do you expect to fly to London (period, question mark) to Paris (period, question mark) to Rome (period, question mark)

   4. **question mark after each** A series of questions.

5. Will you please confirm these reservations before Thursday (period, question mark)

   5. **period** A polite request.

6. What is the name of the new account executive (period, question mark)

   6. **question mark** Direct question.

The Exclamation Point

The exclamation point, like the period and the question mark, is used to show a complete stop in thought. However, its use shows more than a complete stop—the exclamation point is a sign of strong feeling or emotion. It is used after a sentence in which the writer wishes to give a command, to make a plea, or to express surprise or other strong feeling. (Exclamation points are *not* used frequently in business writing.)

Close that window! This is a command. Can't you hear a fellow worker shouting this with strong feeling?

You aren't ready! The writer expresses surprise by using the exclamation point here. Note that if a period were used, the meaning would be changed. The sentence would become a statement of fact, with no strong emotion suggested.

Please try to do better! The exclamation point here expresses a strong emotion —actually a plea.

An exclamation point is also used *after an exclamatory word or phrase*. A sentence that is closely related to such an exclamation is punctuated according to its own meaning. Sometimes an exclamatory word or phrase is a part of an exclamatory sentence. In this case, it is separated from the rest of the sentence by commas.

You gave an inspiring talk. *Congratulations!* The exclamation is the word *congratulations.* The preceding sentence is a statement, correctly followed by a period.

***Help!* The elevator is stuck between floors!** *Help* and the sentence following it are both exclamations and are correctly followed by exclamation points.

***At last!* Are you finally ready?** *At last* is a phrase showing strong feeling. The sentence that follows is a direct question.

Oh! What a day! Both *Oh* and the sentence are exclamations.

But, *oh,* what a relief it is to be finished! *Oh* is an exclamatory word set off with commas because it occurs within a sentence. In this case the entire sentence becomes an exclamation.

🎯 Practice

Select the correct punctuation for the following sentences, and be ready to defend your choices.

1. Good news (period, exclamation point) Our agents can now offer you same-day delivery (period, exclamation point)

   1. exclamation point; exclamation point *or* period The second sentence can be either a statement or an exclamation.

2. Oh (comma, exclamation point) Mr. Dano didn't expect this sort of reaction (period, exclamation point)

   2. exclamation point; period *or* exclamation point *Oh* shows strong feeling and is not part of the sentence that follows; the sentence may be either a statement or an exclamation.

3. What (period, exclamation point) Wasn't that letter mailed on Tuesday (period, question mark, exclamation point)

   3. exclamation point; question mark

4. Never (period, exclamation point) My family and I spend our holidays together (period, exclamation point)

   4. exclamation point; period *Never* expresses strong feeling; the sentence is a declarative statement.

5. What wonderful news (period, exclamation point) You must tell me more about it (period, exclamation point)

   5. exclamation point; period *or* exclamation point An exclamatory phrase and a sentence that may be either a statement or an exclamation.

✷ Assignment

Check your ability to show complete stops in thought by using correctly periods, question marks, and exclamation points in Self-Check 15; then use the Self-Check Key to evaluate your work. In addition, complete Review Sheet 15, and turn it in to your instructor for scoring.

The Comma—Part 1

YOUR OBJECTIVE
To use commas correctly in compound sentences, in series, and after introductory words.

REMEMBER . . .
Punctuation marks guide the reader to follow the thoughts expressed in writing.

The period is used to indicate a full stop — a complete break in thought.

The Comma

While the period indicates a complete stop in thought, the comma acts as a *slow* sign. It tells the reader which words need to be grouped together to make the meaning of the sentence clear. For example, the following sentence is more difficult to read because there are no commas to guide the reader easily into the proper grouping of words.

In the world of business employment is at an all-time high. A comma after *business* would group the words properly so that the reader could grasp their meaning quickly.

In a Compound Sentence

Again, you will recall that a compound sentence is one that contains two or more independent clauses — groups of words that could stand by themselves as sentences. When these clauses are joined by a conjunction (*and, but, or,* or *nor*), a comma should precede the conjunction unless the clauses are very short.

City employees recently received salary increases, and their pension plan was improved. A comma is used before *and,* the conjunction that connects the two independent clauses.

We must raise our prices next year, or we will be forced to operate at a loss. The conjunction *or* connects two independent clauses. The conjunction is correctly preceded by a comma.

We called him but he did not answer. The comma may be omitted before *but* because the two independent clauses are short.

The comma rule just illustrated applies only when conjunctions join independent clauses. When a conjunction is used to join words or phrases that are part of a compound subject or a compound predicate, the conjunction is *not* preceded by a comma.

The Redford Company sold a block of stock and reinvested the capital in building expansion. No comma is used before *and* because the conjunction joins the two verbs of the compound predicate: *sold and reinvested*.

Sales reports from the Denver office and inventory reports from the Cleveland office have always been sent by teletype. The compound subject (*Sales reports and inventory reports*) is connected by *and*. Since *and* does not connect independent clauses, no comma is used before it.

🔆 Practice

Indicate whether a comma, a period, or no punctuation should be inserted in the blank space in each of the following sentences.

1. You have already signed the deed _____ and your property will be transferred.

1. **comma** Two independent clauses joined by *and*.

2. It worked then _____ and it works today.

2. **no punctuation** Both clauses are short.

3. All the damage will be repaired _____ but you must submit itemized bills.

3. **comma** *But* joins two independent clauses.

4. The outdoor lighting system protects against vandalism _____ and improves working conditions.

4. **no punctuation** *And* connects the two parts of a compound predicate—*protects and improves*.

5. Payment was stopped _____ what did you expect?

5. **period** Two independent clauses not joined by a conjunction.

6. Close tolerances must be maintained _____ or assembled units will not function.

6. **comma** The conjunction *or* joins two independent clauses.

7. The oil painting _____ and the watercolor will both be auctioned.

7. **no punctuation** *And* connects two parts of a compound subject.

In a Series

Three or more words, phrases, or clauses in succession are called a *series*. When the last item in the series is preceded by a conjunction, use a comma before the conjunction and between the other items.

Heavy rainfall damaged many *homes, farms, roads,* and *bridges*. Series of words. Note that a comma is used before *and*.

Operating expenses increased 3 percent *in 1960, in 1965,* and again *in 1970*. Series of phrases.

Dictate the report, edit it carefully, and *submit it to Mr. Williams* by Monday. Series of clauses.

The art department will offer the following courses: *lettering, fashion design,* and *advertising and copy layout*. The absence of a comma after *advertising* tells the reader that *advertising and copy layout* is one course.

When *etc.* (meaning "and so forth"), *and so on,* or a similar expression ends a series, use a comma before and a comma after the expression, as in the following examples. As you study the examples, note that the correct abbreviation for "and so forth" is "etc.," not "*and* etc."

> **There is a temporary shortage of butter, milk, eggs, etc., both in and out of the city.** Note the comma both before and after *etc.*
>
> **Wages, working hours, fringe benefits, and so on, are the topics to be discussed.** Note the comma both before and after *and so on.*

If conjunctions are used to join all the items in the series, do not use commas to separate the items.

> **Do you like swimming and boating and fishing?** Note that *and* is used to connect all the items in the series. No comma is needed.

Do not use a comma after the last item in a series unless the sentence structure requires a comma at that point.

> **A jurist, an economist, and an explorer, each known for his or her contribution to society, were the speakers.** Since the parenthetical element *each known for his or her contribution to society* follows the last item in the series, a comma must be used before and after the parenthetical element.

🖊 Practice

Punctuate the following sentences in accordance with what you have learned about punctuation in a series.

1. Electricity telephones and heat are all overhead expenses.

   1. **Electricity, telephones,** Use commas to separate words in a series.

2. Terry assembled the basic data Margaret typed the master copy and Judy made the copies.

   2. **data, . . . copy,** Use commas to separate clauses in a series.

3. Paper clips and staples and rubber cement will all be furnished for the project.

   3. **no commas needed** *And* is used to join the items in the series.

4. Papers books magazines etc. were scattered around the room.

   4. **Papers, books, magazines, etc.,** In the body of a sentence, *etc.* is set off by commas.

5. Checking all invoices statements bills of lading and so on is your responsibility.

   5. **invoices, statements, bills of lading, and so on,** Use commas between items in a series and before and after *and so on.*

6. On Monday on Tuesday and on Wednesday the store will be closed for inventory.

   6. **Monday, on Tuesday,** Use commas to separate a series of phrases.

After an Introductory Word

Use commas to set off introductory words, the most common of which are the following.

accordingly	fortunately	naturally	otherwise
actually	further	next	perhaps
also	however	nevertheless	personally
besides	indeed	no	say
consequently	meanwhile	now	theoretically
finally	moreover	obviously	therefore
first	namely	originally	yes

An introductory word may appear at the beginning of a sentence, or it may introduce a clause within a sentence.

First, let us examine all the facts. Introductory word at the beginning of a sentence.

Production costs are mounting steadily; consequently, prices must be increased. *Consequently* introduces the second independent clause in a compound sentence. (You will learn in Unit 19 about the semicolon used to separate independent clauses joined by such words as *consequently, however,* and *therefore.*)

The words listed as *introductory words* are not always used in an introductory way. Sometimes they modify a word or group of words, in which case they are not followed by a comma. The basic principle of comma use — grouping words together for clarity of meaning — still applies. Study the following examples:

Fortunately, the stock market was high when Mr. Black decided to sell. *Fortunately* is introductory in this sentence. In reading it, note how your voice tends to separate it from the following words.

Fortunately for Mr. Black, the stock market was high when he decided to sell. Here, *fortunately* is an essential part of the phrase *Fortunately for Mr. Black* and should not be followed by a comma. The entire phrase *is* followed by a comma.

After an Introductory Phrase

When a *phrase* — a group of words that does not have *both* a subject and a verb — is used as an introduction to the thought that follows, place a comma after that phrase. Such phrases may be prepositional, participial, or infinitive.

For information about the entire educational program, we invite you to call our local office. Introductory prepositional phrase (*For . . .*).

Seeing little chance for advancement, Charles resigned. Introductory participial phrase (*Seeing . . .*).

To prepare a thorough analysis, you will need every bit of available data. Introductory infinitive phrase (*To prepare . . .*).

Note: If an introductory prepositional phrase is short and flows smoothly into the main thought, do not use a comma. For example: *In the spring we plan to open a branch store.*

After an Introductory Clause

An *introductory clause* is a subordinate clause preceding the main thought, the independent clause. Turn back to Unit 13 to refresh your understanding and review the recognition of subordinate clauses. Common subordinate conjunctions that introduce such clauses are also listed there and should be reviewed. A comma is used to slow the reader after an introductory clause.

> **If you would like to know more about the future of this company, write to the Information Office.** The introductory clause beginning with the subordinate conjunction *if* is followed by a comma.
>
> **While success is not certain, we expect positive results.** *While* clause ends with a comma.

⟡ Practice

In the following sentences, insert commas to set off introductory words, phrases, or clauses.

1. To help students find an answer to their study problems a large library is being organized.

   1. **problems,** Comma after introductory infinitive phrase.

2. Furthermore job needs change as technology continues to develop.

   2. **Furthermore,** Comma after introductory word.

3. In its specialty the Maybury Company excels.

   3. **no comma** Not needed after short introductory phrase.

4. For such essentials as food, clothing, and shelter a substantial part of the income must be set aside.

   4. **shelter,** Comma after an introductory phrase.

5. When employment requirements are listed ability to get along with others is usually included.

   5. **listed,** Comma after introductory clause.

6. A long apprenticeship is unnecessary; however some on-the-job training is essential in the preparation of workers.

   6. **however,** Comma after introductory word in second clause.

⇄ Assignment

Check your ability to use commas correctly in compound sentences, in series, and after introductory words by doing Self-Check 16; then use the Self-Check Key to evaluate your work. In addition, complete Review Sheet 16, and turn it in to your instructor for scoring.

The Comma—Part 2

YOUR OBJECTIVE
To use commas correctly to set off interrupting words, phrases, or clauses within a sentence.

REMEMBER . . .
Punctuation marks guide the reader to follow the thoughts expressed in writing.

Commas slow down the reader after introductory words, phrases, and clauses and before conjunctions that connect independent clauses.

Nonrestrictive Words

Words that can be omitted from a sentence without affecting the clarity of the message are *nonrestrictive* (unnecessary) and are set off from the rest of the sentence by commas. Nonrestrictive words indicate to the reader the parts of the message that are closely related—but not absolutely necessary—to the main thought. However, words that are *restrictive* (necessary to the meaning of the sentence) are not set off by commas.

It is important to remember that when commas set off words that could be omitted without changing the meaning of the sentence, the commas are used both before *and* after the nonrestrictive words. Of course, if the unnecessary words occur at the end of the sentence, a period or other end punctuation mark takes the place of the second comma.

The comma is used with three kinds of nonrestrictive words or expressions: *interrupting, parenthetical,* and *explanatory.* Keep in mind the basic rule that all words not absolutely necessary to the meaning of a sentence are set off by commas.

With Interrupting Words and Phrases

Use commas to set off a word or phrase that interrupts a sentence without contributing to its meaning.

> **The city income tax, however, became effective in 1970.** *However* can be omitted without changing the meaning of the sentence and is set off by commas.

> **A main concern, of course, is to determine the most urgent reforms.** *Of course* is set off by commas because it is not essential to the meaning of the sentence.

There are many words and phrases that are commonly used as "interrupters." Here are some of those that you will see most frequently:

as always	nevertheless
consequently	of course
for example	on the other hand
however	to say the least
moreover	therefore

These words and phrases are set off by commas when used as interrupters.

With Parenthetical Phrases and Clauses

An expression inserted in a sentence as a comment is called a parenthetical expression *if the meaning of the sentence is complete without it.* Parenthetical phrases and clauses may add emphasis, point out contrast, or slightly modify the original statement. In any case, parenthetical expressions are not essential to the meaning and are set off by commas.

The discussion, everyone was willing to concede, had reached a logical conclusion. The clause *everyone was willing to concede* qualifies the message. You will note, however, that you can omit these words and still have a message that is clear. Therefore, this parenthetical expression is set off by commas.

We plan to rent a mountain home, or at least a cabin, for one month for our top sales representative. Note the amending words *or at least a cabin.* When you omit this phrase from the sentence, you do not affect the clarity of the sentence.

The figures must be proofread carefully, not just glanced at quickly, if the final report is to be accurate. *Not just glanced at quickly* expresses a contrasting thought that may be omitted without changing the main thought. Therefore, commas are correctly used both before and after the expression.

✎ Practice

See whether you can identify words and expressions that should be set off by commas because they are not necessary to the meaning of the sentence. Insert commas wherever necessary.

1. Our company will of course stand behind our guarantee.
   1. , of course,

2. The new computer it is generally agreed will cut payroll production time in half.
   2. , it is generally agreed,

3. All stenographers not clerks will receive a pay increase this month.
   3. , not clerks,

4. Shipments however will not be delayed by the steel shortage.
   4. , however,

5. Restrictions regarding credit as you can well imagine affect installment buying.
   5. , as you can well imagine,

6. Posture chairs are desirable for but not absolutely necessary to the comfort of the typists.
   6. , but not absolutely necessary to,

With Explanatory Clauses

In the previous examples in this unit, the words interrupting the main thought of the sentence were quite clear, making it easy to decide where to place commas. Sometimes explanatory groups of words are more difficult to punctuate correctly because they may or may not be necessary for the meaning of the sentence. *If they are not necessary,* they are set off by commas; otherwise, no commas are used.

Ms. Hammond, *who has had many years' experience in the shoe business,* **will join our staff next month.** You can omit the words set off by commas and still have a sentence that makes perfect sense: *Ms. Hammond will join our staff next month.* The words set off by commas are explanatory—they give additional information.

The sales representative *who joined our staff this month* **has had many years' experience in the shoe business.** No commas are used in this sentence because all the words are necessary for clear meaning. If you cut out *who joined our staff this month,* you would not know *which* sales representative.

Besides the word *who,* the words *that* and *which* are also used to introduce explanatory clauses. *Who,* of course, refers to people. *That* and *which* both refer to places or things; however, careful writers make a distinction between their use in parenthetical or explanatory clauses. Clauses that are *not* necessary to the meaning of the sentence are introduced by *which,* and clauses that *are* necessary are introduced by *that.*

All blueprints that are filed have been approved by the contractor. The word *that* introduces the clause *that are filed.* No commas are used because the clause is necessary for clarity.

The yellow lounge chair, which is slightly soiled, will be included in the clearance sale. The word *which* introduces a clause *not* necessary to the meaning of the sentence. Thus the clause, *which is slightly soiled,* is set off by commas.

✍ Practice

Indicate where commas are needed to set off words that are not essential to the meaning of the sentence.

1. Stores in Florida and California where temperatures are mild have no demand for heavy fur coats.

   1. **, where temperatures are mild,** Additional information.

2. Stores in states where temperatures are mild have no demand for heavy fur coats.

   2. **Correct** *Where temperatures are mild* is needed to identify *which* states "have no demand for heavy fur coats."

3. The deadline date which was announced last month is August 1.

   3. **, which was announced last month,** Note the use of *which* to introduce an explanatory clause that can be omitted.

4. The deadline date that we must meet is the one announced last month.

   4. **Correct** Without the *that* clause, the sentence would have no clear meaning.

5. The results of the test mailing are as disappointing as the sales manager expected them to be.

6. The results of the test mailing are disappointing as the sales manager expected them to be.

5. **Correct** The clause *as disappointing as the sales manager expected them to be* is essential to the meaning.

6. **disappointing,** A comma is correctly used before the nonrestrictive clause at the end of the sentence.

With Appositives

In Unit 6 you studied the correct case form for appositives. You already know, then, that an appositive is set off by commas, that it gives additional information, and that it means the same thing as the word or words with which it is in apposition.

There are instances where appositives are not set off by commas because the terms are very closely connected. If the word or words in apposition can be omitted without affecting the meaning of the sentence, they should be set off by commas. If they are necessary to the meaning, they should not be set off.

> **Our representative, Mr. Jason Carter, will demonstrate our product.** The message is clear if the appositive, *Mr. Jason Carter,* is omitted; therefore, commas are correctly used.

> **Mary's brother Jim has recently joined her advertising agency.** If you omit *Jim,* your reader will not know which brother you mean. Since *Jim* is necessary for identification, it is not set off by commas.

With Degrees

A degree such as *M.D.* or *Ph.D.* used after a person's name gives additional information about that person. The *M.D.* tells you the person is a doctor of medicine. The *Ph.D.* tells you the person is a doctor of philosophy. Degrees are set off by commas.

> **The consultant is Pauline DeLoche, Ph.D., a well-known authority in the field of space science.** *Ph.D.,* a degree, is correctly set off by commas.

With Titles and Other Explanatory Terms

Jr. after a person's name or *Inc.* or *Ltd.* after a company name tells you more about the person or the company. In the past, such titles or explanatory terms were always set off by commas. However, the trend today is to omit the commas. In any case, the best rule is to follow the person's or the company's preference when you know what it is.

> **Peter Greco Jr. established the Greco Construction Company Inc. in 1962.** No commas are used before or after *Jr.* or *Inc.,* following the current trend. However, commas would be correct *before* and *after Jr.* if the individual himself writes it that way. Also, a comma *before* and *after Inc.* would be correct if the company letterhead lists it that way.

With Calendar Dates, Cities, and States

Whenever the year is included in a date or the name of a city is followed by the state, set off the year or the state by one comma if it occurs at the end of a sentence and two commas if it occurs inside a sentence. Note the exception in the second example.

> **On April 1, 1970, I moved from Springfield, Illinois, to San Francisco.** Commas correctly set off *1970,* the year, from the month and day; and they set off *Illinois,* the state, from the city.

> **The manuscript was ready by May 1977 for publication the next year.** Commas may be used to set off the year in this sentence, but the trend is to omit both commas when the day is omitted between the month and the year.

Practice

Study these sentences and decide where commas are necessary.

1. The first applicant Miss Jane Thaler was not qualified for the job.

1. **, Miss Jane Thaler,** Nonessential appositive.

2. Our office in Gary Indiana will arrange for reservations.

2. **Gary, Indiana,** Set off the state from the city by commas.

3. Jack has arranged for the August 1988 meeting to be held in Detroit.

3. **Correct** The year need not be set off by commas when the day is omitted.

4. Amanda Blake D.D.S. has just opened a new office.

4. **Blake, D.D.S.,** Degree written after a name.

5. The caller an elderly gentleman was ushered into the president's office.

5. **, an elderly gentleman,** Nonessential appositive.

6. The author Thomas Bolter was honored by the Kiwanis Club.

6. **Correct** Essential appositive.

Assignment

Check your ability to use commas correctly to set off interrupting words, phrases, or clauses by doing Self-Check 17; then use the Self-Check Key to evaluate your work. In addition, complete Review Sheet 17, and turn it in to your instructor for scoring.

The Comma—Part 3

YOUR OBJECTIVE

To use the comma correctly with two or more adjectives, words in direct address, and numbers; to use the comma to indicate omitted words.

REMEMBER . . .

The comma is a "slow down" sign that helps the reader to interpret your message easily and clearly.

With Adjectives

When two or more adjectives separately modify the same noun, use commas to separate the adjectives. As you study the following example sentences, notice these important details:

1. A comma is correctly used between adjectives when it takes the place of *and.*
2. No comma is used between the *last* adjective and the word modified.
3. No comma is used between adjectives that do not *separately* modify the same word.

> **Juan Raymon is a prosperous, well-liked citizen.** *Prosperous* modifies *citizen; well-liked* modifies *citizen.* Notice that the comma takes the place of *and* between *prosperous* and *well-liked.*
>
> **The buyer searched for stylish winter coats.** *Stylish* and *winter* do not *separately* modify *coats.* You would not say "a stylish and winter coat." Therefore, no comma is used between the two modifiers.

✐ Practice

Decide whether commas are needed between the modifiers in the following sentences. Remember not to place a comma between the last adjective and the word modified.

1. Sales advertising and display procedures are being studied carefully.

   1. **Sales, advertising,** Sales *and* advertising *and . . .*

2. Shopworn defective goods cannot be offered for sale in this store.

   2. **Shopworn,** Shopworn *and* defective.

3. Mrs. Wilson is a quick-thinking but slow-moving person.

   3. **Correct** The modifiers are joined by the conjunction *but.*

88

4. The supervisor requested an accurate comprehensive up-to-date report.

4. **accurate, comprehensive,** Accurate *and* comprehensive *and* up-to-date.

5. The article was written by a famous advertising executive.

5. **Correct** You would not say "famous *and* advertising executive."

To Indicate Omissions

Sometimes words may be omitted from a sentence without confusing the reader. Generally, such words are omitted to avoid needless repetition. When an omission occurs, a comma is normally used to slow down the reader and point out the omission.

> **Shoes will be on sale for $12.95; slippers, for $4.99.** The comma after *slippers* slows down the reader and stands for the clearly understood words *will be on sale.*
>
> **Mr. Elam dictated four memos; Mrs. Hackett, six.** In the second clause the verb *dictated* is omitted and replaced by a comma.

In Direct Address

Names or terms used in speaking directly to particular persons are said to be used in direct address. Such names or terms are set off by commas.

> **You, Mr. West, are the newly elected president.** Speaking directly to *Mr. West.*
> **It is my pleasure, members of the Garden Club, to offer you an unusual technique for flower arrangement.** Speaking directly to *members of the Garden Club.*
> **Please notice, my dear friend, that these tickets are complimentary.** Speaking directly to someone addressed as *my dear friend.*

🎵 Practice

Clarify your understanding of comma usage in direct address or to indicate omission of words by punctuating the following sentences.

1. Will you show me how to use the copy machine Jim?

1. **machine, Jim?** Direct address.

2. In September sales increased 4 percent; in October 10 percent; and in November 12 percent.

2. **October, ... November,** To indicate omission of *sales increased.*

3. You sir are invited to the special meeting of the Board of Directors.

3. **You, sir,** Direct address.

4. Something has been omitted. What I cannot say just now.

4. **What,** Omission of *has been omitted.*

5. The walnut table costs $100; the mahogany $90; and the maple $80.

5. **mahogany, . . . maple,** Omission of *costs.*

In Repeated Expressions

A thought may be repeated to emphasize an idea. Such a repetition should be set off by commas.

> Barbara's daughter is talented, very talented.
> The children appeared bored, bored, bored.

In Numbers and Between Unrelated Numbers

In numbers of four or more digits, use commas to separate hundreds from thousands, thousands from millions, and so on. Also, use a comma to separate two unrelated numbers when they are written together.

> Attendance at the charity ball was 2,456; receipts were over $10,500, which brings total contributions to $2,450,090. The commas separate hundreds from thousands and thousands from millions.

> In 1977, 1,250 employees were participating in the retirement plan. The comma between *1977* and *1,250* separates the two numbers and reduces the possibility of confusion.

Do not use a comma when writing years, page numbers, house numbers, telephone numbers, serial numbers, decimals, or ZIP Code numbers.

in 1971	Phone: 873-4211	*pi* equals 3.1416
page 1230	Policy 621432	Ames, Iowa 50010
4420 Wells Avenue		

𝄞 Practice

Can you tell where to place commas in the following sentences?

1. Try try to make a perfect typewritten copy.

   1. **Try, try** Word repeated for emphasis.

2. For item 49 2427 people requested copies.

   2. **49, 2,427** Between two unrelated numbers and in a number of four figures.

3. His policy number as of 1977 is 43728.

   3. **Correct** No commas in year or serial numbers.

4. Of the total tax of $64276 $61000 has already been paid.

   4. **$64,276, $61,000** Commas needed to separate two unrelated numbers and in numbers of four or more figures.

5. Mr. Byrnes is wealthy exceedingly wealthy.

   5. **wealthy, exceedingly wealthy** Repeated expression.

⇄ Assignment

Check your ability to use commas correctly with two or more adjectives, with words in direct address, with numbers, and to indicate omitted words by doing Self-Check 18; then use the Self-Check Key to evaluate your work. In addition, complete Review Sheet 18, and turn it in to your instructor for scoring.

The Semicolon, the Colon, and the Dash

YOUR OBJECTIVE
To know the functions of the semicolon, the colon, and the dash as partial stop signs within complete thoughts; and to use them correctly in your writing.

REMEMBER...
Knowing the framework of the sentence provides the basis for your study of punctuation.

Each punctuation mark serves a particular purpose in guiding the reader to interpret your written message easily and clearly.

Semicolon

You have already studied the elements of sentence structure that are basic to your understanding of semicolon use:

1. A compound sentence is one that contains two or more independent clauses—clauses that could stand alone as complete sentences.
2. The independent clauses in a compound sentence are usually connected by a coordinate conjunction (*and, but, or,* or *nor*) or a correlative conjunction (*not only . . . but also, either . . . or,* etc.).
3. A comma usually comes before the conjunction that connects the independent clauses in a compound sentence.

The following sentence will help you to review the principles that you have already studied.

The shipment was sent on November 12, but it was not received until early in December. This sentence is made up of two independent clauses. A comma separates the two clauses and precedes the connective word, *but.*

As in the above illustration, a comma is usually the correct punctuation between the independent clauses in a compound sentence. However, there are times when the semicolon is needed.

1. When the independent clauses in a compound sentence are not connected by a conjunction, use a semicolon to separate those clauses.

The incident occurred at two o'clock; it was not reported until four. Since the clauses are not joined by a conjunction, a semicolon is used to separate them.
Ms. Harris is president of the company; Mr. Harrison is the general manager; Dr. Ferris is the vice president. No conjunctions connect these three closely related thoughts; semicolons are used to separate the clauses.

2. In some compound sentences, the second independent clause starts with an introductory word, such as *however, consequently, therefore.* You will remember from your study in Unit 16 that a comma is used following such introductory words. Now, as in the sentences below, use a semicolon before these words when they introduce the second independent clause.

> **The accounting procedures have been revised; however, your work will remain unchanged.** Since the second clause is introduced by *however,* a semicolon is used to separate the clauses. Note the comma that follows *however.*

> **Mr. Bates must complete a rush job today; consequently, Miss Jordan will work with him for a few hours.** *Consequently* introduces the second independent clause, and the semicolon precedes it.

3. When one or more of the independent clauses in a compound sentence contains a comma, use a semicolon to separate the clauses if using a comma might result in misreading. If no misreading is likely, a comma is sufficient.

> **We ordered stencils, staples, and carbon paper; and Ditto masters, paper clips, and thumbtacks were sent instead.** To avoid confusion, a semicolon is used to separate these two independent clauses joined by *and.*

> **Mrs. Stone, chairman of the committee, bought the invitations, and several members of the committee helped her prepare and mail them.** Even though the first clause contains commas, a comma before the conjunction *and* is sufficient to separate the two independent clauses.

4. When two independent clauses are connected by *for example, for instance, namely, that is,* or a similar transitional expression, use a semicolon before the transitional expression.

> **The survey was very successful; that is, more than 70 percent of those receiving the questionnaire completed and returned it.** Note the semicolon before and the comma after the transitional expression *that is.*

Also, use a semicolon before a transitional expression when the first part of the sentence expresses the complete thought and an explanation is added almost as an afterthought.

> **When you transcribe the letter, don't forget to add reference initials; for example, JRC/RMH or JRC:RMH.**

5. If one or more items in a series contains commas, use a semicolon to separate the items in the series.

> **Sales conferences will be held in Houston, Texas; Washington, D.C.; and Raleigh, North Carolina.** The items in this series of city and state names are separated by semicolons.

🎵 Practice

Is a comma or a semicolon the correct punctuation mark for the blank in each of the following sentences? Give reasons for your choice.

1. The machines in the production room are in constant demand _____ for example, the photocopier is used by 30 people a day.

1. semicolon The transitional expression *for example* links two independent clauses.

2. Take a careful look at the outline _____ you may wish to make extensive changes.

3. Several details are missing _____ but if you wish, I'll start typing the report.

4. The invoices are dated May 3, 1976 _____ June 14, 1977 _____ and June 20, 1977.

5. The original idea was simple _____ but the action was complicated.

6. We specialize in shoes of unusual sizes _____ for example, 13AAA and 14B.

2. **semicolon** No conjunction between independent clauses.

3. **comma** No misreading is likely.

4. **semicolon, semicolon** Items in the series contain commas.

5. **comma** Compound sentence connected by coordinate conjunction.

6. **semicolon** Explanation is an afterthought.

Colon

The colon tells the reader that what follows deserves special consideration. You already know that a colon is used after the salutation of a business letter (for example, *Dear Mrs. Brown:* or *Gentlemen:*). You also know that a colon is used to separate hours from minutes in writing time; for example, *3:45 p.m.* Other uses of the colon are discussed and illustrated here.

1. Use a colon after a statement that introduces a list or an enumeration. The words *as follows, the following, this, those,* and *thus* often precede the list or enumeration.

   To stimulate committee action, a group needs the following characteristics: a good leader, a definite goal, and interested committee members.

   In the above example, the items that follow the colon are included as part of the sentence. They may also be enumerated and displayed on separate lines, as in the following example:

   The person who will be hired for the secretarial position must have the following personal characteristics:
   1. Poise
   2. Tact
   3. Self-reliance

2. Use a colon before a list or a complete sentence if you wish to make the list or sentence stand out as important. Capitalize the first word of a complete sentence following a colon (a) if you wish to emphasize the sentence, (b) if the sentence states a formal rule, (c) if what follows is a quoted sentence, or (d) if what follows are two or more sentences.

   Let's remember our primary goal: We must help provide the residents of our community with the health, safety, and educational services they require. Capital for emphasis.

   The most important spelling rule is this one: If you are not sure, look it up! Capital for formal rule.

   A colon tells the reader this: "Here is something that I must read carefully." Capital for quoted sentence.

We agreed to both suggestions: We should first define the primary market for this product. Once we have done so, we should then obtain up-to-date mailing lists. Capital for each of two sentences following colon.

3. If the last words in a sentence do not lead *directly* into a list or a statement, use a period—not a colon—to end the sentence.

If you keep these suggestions in mind, you will be able to stretch your buying dollar. (1) Prepare and use shopping lists. (2) Examine articles carefully before buying them. (3) Consider upkeep and repair costs of major items. The words immediately preceding the list are not the ones that introduce it. If the words *these suggestions* appeared closer to the end of the sentence, a colon would be used. The same principle applies when such lists are enumerated and displayed on separate lines.

Practice

What punctuation mark is needed for the blanks in the following sentences? Give the reason for each choice.

1. The order specified clearly the following factors _____ the width of the curtains, the length of the draperies, and the size of the fixtures.

   1. colon   Before a list.

2. You must consider three factors _____ distance from the warehouse, means of transportation, and availability of qualified employees.

   2. colon   Before a list.

3. A new training course, as described in the accompanying outline, will be tried experimentally with our sales staff _____

   3. period   The last part of the sentence does not lead directly into the outline.

4. Before going on the staff skiing party, I must buy the following items _____
   1. Boots
   2. Ski jacket
   3. Gloves

   4. colon   Before an enumerated, displayed list.

5. Mr. Bade insists on only one thing _____ Employees must report to work on time.

   5. colon   Before a complete sentence that the writer wishes to emphasize.

Dash

The dash is another partial stop signal. The writer may use it to change the thought abruptly or to insert *parenthetical* items—items that can be omitted without affecting the sense of the sentence. Overusing the dash should be avoided, but it is especially effective for cutting off the message abruptly and making the words that follow the dash more emphatic.

1. When it would be correct to use a colon, a semicolon, or a dash, use a dash if you want to achieve the greatest emphasis.

   The top drawer contains stationery supplies; namely, letterheads, envelopes, carbon paper, and second sheets. The semicolon and the word *namely* tell the reader that a list is coming almost as an afterthought.

   The top drawer contains stationery supplies—letterheads, envelopes, carbon paper, and second sheets. The use of the dash, with no introductory word, makes the listing more forceful.

2. Use a dash to give special emphasis to a summarizing statement or to a repeated statement.

   The monotonous checking operations, the tiresome copying and recopying, the constant addition of new material—all were forgotten when the finished report was so enthusiastically received. The "punch line" summary of the drudgeries —*all were forgotten when the finished report was so enthusiastically received*— is made more conspicuous by the dash.

   Thanks! I appreciated your informative letter—an extremely informative letter, indeed. The dash before the repetition—*an extremely informative letter, indeed* —makes this the outstanding idea in the sentence.

3. Use a dash instead of a comma or a semicolon before the last item in a series when you wish to give it special significance.

   Miss Longet read the request, checked the dollar figures—and signed it. The dash gives special significance to the fact that Miss Longet signed the request.

4. Also, use a dash to give special emphasis to an afterthought, to soften a statement that might be offensive, or to prepare the reader for some topic that will be discussed later.

   Here's a handsome new poster—printed in four colors! Dash to emphasize an afterthought.

   We are returning your manuscript—even though we think it has a great deal of merit. Dash to soften a statement of refusal.

   The budget requires considerable revision—but we will discuss that tomorrow. Dash to prepare the reader for a topic that will be discussed later.

Other Punctuation Used With Dashes

There are several principles governing punctuation of material enclosed in dashes. Study the following examples and the principles that they illustrate.

You said—so I have heard—that you favor lowering our list price. A dash may be used in place of a comma both before and after parenthetical material in a sentence.

What response is expected—a "Yes" or a "No"? Whenever material set off by a dash ends a sentence, the regular end-of-sentence punctuation is used. In this example, the sentence is a question that correctly ends in a question mark.

Many parents—and Alice and Craig, of course, are no exceptions—are concerned with the low education budget. Commas are used where needed within the material that is set off by dashes; thus *of course* is set off by commas.

Miss Garcia asked—didn't she?—whether you would serve on the hospitality committee. The question mark and the exclamation point are the *only* punctuation marks that are used *before* the ending dash.

Here are imported ties—yes, think of it!—for only $3.50. An exclamation point is used correctly before the ending dash.

🎗 Practice

In the following sentences, decide where you would place dashes and why.

1. Two guards were on duty no, there were three.

   1. **duty—no** Afterthought.

2. Our trustees Mr. Kowalski, Mrs. Archer, and Mr. McCloy are planning a novel investment program.

   2. **trustees—Mr. Kowalski . . . Mr. McCloy—are** Parenthetical.

3. You can cook an entire meal steak, corn, and potatoes on this outdoor grill.

   3. **meal—steak . . . potatoes—on** Explanatory.

4. This opportunity one that no one can resist will inspire our sales force.

   4. **opportunity—one . . . resist—will** Parenthetical.

5. Tickets can be purchased at the box office yes, also at the downtown music store.

   5. **box office—yes** Afterthought.

6. Tennis, skiing, and skating these are their favorite sports.

   6. **skating—these** Summarizing statement.

✹ Assignment

Check your ability to use the semicolon, colon, and dash correctly by doing Self-Check 19; then use the Self-Check Key to evaluate your work. In addition, complete Review Sheet 19, and turn it in to your instructor for scoring.

Quotation Marks

YOUR OBJECTIVE
To use quotation marks correctly to show exact words written or spoken by someone else, quoted expressions, and titles.

REMEMBER . . .
Punctuation marks guide the reader to understand your written message easily and clearly.

Direct Quotations

When you record word for word what someone else has said or written, use quotation marks to enclose the exact words written or spoken by that person. Use a comma to set off a short direct quotation that comes at the beginning or at the end of a sentence.

> **The advertising directors announced, "A special direct-mail campaign will begin in March."** Note the comma after *announced.*

> **"A special direct-mail campaign will begin in March," the advertising director announced.** Note that the comma appears after *March,* the last word in the quotation in this sentence.

If the direct quotation is long or is introduced by an independent clause, use a colon—not a comma—before the quotation.

> **Miss Johnson stated: "If Mr. Fine completes the first draft of the contract by noon, I will be able to type it by five. If he doesn't, I'll have to type it tomorrow."** Colon before long quotation.

> **Mrs. Sutton said this: "The report must be completed by next Monday."** Colon before quotation introduced by an independent clause.

If a direct quotation is interrupted, place quotation marks around the quoted words only and use commas to separate the quotation from the rest of the sentence.

> **"Not a bad profit," my partner said, "for a company that was organized only a year ago."** The interruption is *my partner said,* and it is separated from the quotation by commas.

Remember that quotation marks are not used with an indirect quotation, that is, a restatement of someone else's words. As illustrated below, an indirect quotation is often introduced by *that* or *whether.*

> **The advertising director announced that a special direct-mail campaign will begin in March.** This sentence contains a restatement of a direct quotation. The sentence can be written as a direct quote as follows: *The advertising director announced, "A special direct-mail campaign will begin in March."*

Practice

Insert quotation marks and commas or colons where needed in the following sentences.

1. I see complained Margaret that there are no envelopes.

1. "I see," . . . Margaret, "that . . . envelopes." Interrupted quotation.

2. Why they should have the contract is more than I can understand Mr. Edwards said.

2. "Why . . . understand," Comma because the quotation does not end the sentence.

3. My boss said Miss Kovac, I would like you to meet Mr. Bingham.

3. said, "Miss Kovac, I . . . Bingham." Comma after expression introducing a short quotation.

4. The division manager reported that he will be in Dallas on Tuesday.

4. Correct Indirect quotation.

5. The general manager issued this directive Report all thefts immediately upon discovery of loss.

5. directive: "Report . . . loss." Colon after independent clause introducing a quotation.

Quoted Expressions and Terms

Some expressions and terms are enclosed in quotation marks to signal to the reader that the quoted words have special significance.

1. Words and phrases introduced by such expressions as *so-called, marked, signed,* and *entitled* are enclosed in quotation marks.

   Can you give an example of their so-called "hands off" policy?
   The package was marked "Fragile."

2. Words referred to as words may be underscored (italicized in printed material) or enclosed in quotation marks.

   Either <u>and</u> or <u>but</u> could be used in that sentence. *Or* Either "and" or "but" could . . .
   To improve your diction, practice pronouncing the "t's" in these words. *Or* the <u>t</u>'s.

3. Technical or trade terms that may be unfamiliar to the reader are enclosed in quotation marks when they are first introduced.

   Newspaper "cuts" are the property of the newspaper using them. *Cut* is a technical term meaning "an engraved block or plate for printing."
   This new locomotive will make it possible to eliminate "pushers" on the westbound grade. *Pusher* is a term peculiar to railroading in this sentence.

4. A word or phrase that is formally defined is usually underscored (italicized in printed material), and its definition is usually placed in quotation marks.

   In the printing industry, a <u>signature</u> is "a large sheet of paper that is printed and folded (usually to 32 pages)."

5. Slang, humorous words, and poor grammar purposely used to make writing more interesting are enclosed in quotation marks.

> The speaker told a heckler to "cool it."
> He took the visitors into his "inner sanctum."
> Those rumors simply "ain't so."

6. Translations of foreign words are enclosed in quotation marks; the foreign words themselves are underscored (italicized in printed material).

> Adieu means "goodbye."
> "Let the buyer beware" is the translation of the Latin words caveat emptor.

✍ Practice

Correctly punctuate the following sentences. Not all sentences will require additional punctuation.

1. The term automotive is used frequently in our trade magazine.

1. "automotive" *or* automotive

2. The words bring and take are sometimes confused.

2. "bring" and "take" *or* bring and take

3. Please check and double-check all typewritten work.

3. Correct

4. The package was marked Handle With Care.

4. "Handle With Care."

5. *Et cetera* is the Latin term for and so forth.

5. "and so forth."

Quotations Within Quotations

A quotation within a quotation is enclosed in single quotation marks. On a typewriter, the single quotation mark is the same as the apostrophe.

> The young woman replied, "We must remember that what he calls 'net price' is not the price paid by the consumer."
>
> "Try to collect," Mr. Norton wrote, "all accounts I have marked 'past due.' "
> Note that the period is inside both the single and the double quotation marks when a quotation within a quotation comes at the end of a sentence.

Quoting Titles

Use quotation marks to enclose titles of lectures, short poems, articles, essays, parts and chapters of books, songs, radio and TV programs. Use quotation marks also for mottoes and toasts.

> "Writing Effective Sales Letters" appears in Part II, which is entitled "Written Communications." Title of a chapter and title of a section of a book.
>
> The speaker's topic was "Look to Tomorrow." Title of a talk.

Although they are frequently used as titles of parts of books, such terms as *preface, appendix, contents,* and *index* are not enclosed in quotation marks. However, such terms are often capitalized.

> **The main topics covered in this text are summarized in the Preface.**
>
> **A list of commonly used abbreviations appears in the Appendix.**

The titles of books, magazines, newspapers, long poems, and other works that are published and bound separately and the titles of plays, movies, operas, and paintings are not enclosed in quotation marks. Such titles are usually underscored (italicized in printed material). In some cases, however, they are typed in all-capital letters, either to avoid using underscores too frequently or to provide additional emphasis.

> **Jon Meridith wrote the novel <u>Light of Day</u>.** *Or* **LIGHT OF DAY** *or Light of Day.*
>
> **We ran an ad in <u>The New York Times</u>.** *Or* **THE NEW YORK TIMES** *or The New York Times.*
>
> **<u>My Fair Lady</u> was a successful Broadway play.** *Or* **MY FAIR LADY** *or My Fair Lady.*

⑰ Practice

Use quotation marks where they are needed in these sentences. Watch also for quotes within quotes and for other punctuation problems.

1. Have you read the latest issue of Time?

   1. <u>Time</u>   Name of magazine.

2. Do you have tickets to see the modern-dress performance of Hamlet?

   2. <u>Hamlet</u>?   Name of a play.

3. Business first is her favorite motto.

   3. "Business first"   A motto.

4. Mrs. Nelson repeated, I have not read your article The Age of Automation

   4. "I . . . article, 'The Age of Automation.'"   Quote within a quote.

5. My favorite newspaper is the Morning Times.

   5. <u>Morning Times</u>   Name of newspaper.

Punctuation at End of Quoted Material

Punctuation marks at the end of quoted words, phrases, and sentences are written in the order indicated below.

1. *Periods and commas* are always placed *inside* the closing quotation mark.

   > **The desired response most certainly is "Yes."** *Period* is placed *inside* closing quotation mark.
   >
   > **"Please notify the vendor at once," the purchasing agent ordered.** *Comma* is placed *inside* closing quotation mark.

2. *Colons and semicolons* are always placed *outside* the closing quotation mark.

   > **The following are listed under "Assets": cash, equipment, and accounts receivable.** *Colon* is placed *outside* the closing quotation mark.

The person who is being sued is known as the "defendant"; the one who is bringing the suit, as the "plaintiff." Note that the *semicolon* is placed *outside,* but the *period* is placed *inside,* the closing quotation mark.

3. *Question marks and exclamation points* may be placed inside or outside closing quotation marks, depending on the following conditions:

If only the quoted words are a question or an exclamation, the question mark or the exclamation point is placed *inside* the closing quotation mark.

You heard him ask, "What time does the store close?" Here the question mark applies only to the quoted material and logically goes *inside* the closing quotation mark.

Mrs. Fasano shouted "Congratulations!" from across the room. Since the exclamation point applies only to the quotation, it must be placed with the quoted word—*inside* the closing quotation mark.

If the *entire* sentence, not just the quotation, is a question or an exclamation, the question mark or the exclamation point is placed *outside* the closing quotation mark.

Why did you label the folder "correspondence"? Here the question mark is *not* a part of the quotation. It marks the end of a sentence that asks a question; therefore, it is placed *outside* the closing quotation mark.

How careless of you to drop a package marked "Fragile"! Here the entire sentence is an exclamation, and the exclamation mark is placed *after* the word within quotation marks.

🎵 Practice

Place quotation and other necessary punctuation marks where they are needed in the following sentences. Be able to tell why you punctuate as you do.

1. Take advantage of my offer Chris joked. You need help.

1. "Take . . . offer," . . . . "You need help." Interrupted quotation.

2. The personnel director inquired Are all part-time openings now filled

2. inquired, "Are . . . filled?" Question mark placed inside closing quotation mark because it applies only to the quoted material.

3. Our specialists have "know-how" in addition, they have common sense.

3. "know-how"; Semicolon is always outside the closing quotation.

4. Ms. Rand said that the offer was no longer open.

4. Correct Indirect quotation needs no quotation marks.

5. Is this stock what is known as a "blue chip"

5. "blue chip"? The entire sentence is a question; thus the question mark is written outside the closing quotation mark.

6. The manager said I very much regret the decision

6. said, "I . . . decision." Direct quote.

✻ Assignment

Check your ability to use correctly quotation marks and other punctuation related to their use by doing Self-Check 20; then use the Self-Check Key to evaluate your work. In addition, complete Review Sheet 20, and turn it in to your instructor for scoring.

Parentheses and the Apostrophe

YOUR OBJECTIVE
To use parentheses correctly—especially when used with other punctuation marks; and to use the apostrophe correctly to show contractions, omissions, and "coined" verbs.

REMEMBER . . .
Punctuation marks guide the reader to understand your written thoughts clearly and easily.

Commas and dashes are used to set off words that give additional information.

The apostrophe is used with nouns to show possession and to form the plurals of letters, symbols, signs, and words used as words.

Parentheses for Words That Give Additional Information

In addition to commas and dashes, parentheses are also used to enclose words that give additional information. However, each mark serves a distinct purpose. Parentheses are properly used to enclose material added to a sentence merely as a supplementary detail or as an afterthought. By using parentheses, the writer is signaling the reader that the information enclosed in the parentheses is not too important—it is added just in case it might be needed—and does not change the main thought.

A real estate mortgage is a written document that pledges title to real property (land and buildings) as security for debts. *Land and buildings* is added to be sure that the reader understands what is meant by *real property*. The words make no addition, however, to the *main thought* of the sentence.

You will receive 10 percent off (our usual cash discount) if you pay within ten days. The supplementary words *our usual cash discount* do not change the main thought.

Parentheses in Enumerations

Parentheses are used to enclose letters or figures that precede enumerations within sentences. In addition, subdivisions in outlines are often enclosed in parentheses (see Unit 14).

> **Please follow these instructions: (1) complete the application, (2) write a check or money order for the required amount, and (3) send both in the enclosed addressed envelope.** Note the use of the colon before the list and the commas in the series.

> **1. You will need the following: (a) a box of paper clips, (b) a stapler, (c) felt-tip pens, and (d) construction paper.** Letters are used to enumerate items within a sentence when the sentence itself is part of a *numbered* sequence. Note that periods are not used after numbers or letters in parentheses.

Parentheses for References

Use parentheses to enclose a reference, a direction, or the name of an authority for a statement.

> **Efficiency is production without waste (Webster).** The sentence is taken directly from a definition given in a dictionary.

> **A well-known adage is "A penny saved is a penny earned" (Franklin).** The reader will understand that Franklin coined the adage.

> **Sales increased 10 percent over last year (see attached report), but profits continued to decline.** The words in parentheses tell the reader where to find detailed information.

🖊 Practice

In the following sentences, insert parentheses where needed. Be able to give the reason for the marks that you use.

1. In this firm the position of comptroller chief accountant requires a CPA degree.

   1. (chief accountant) To indicate additional information.

2. Most of us received the usual raise about 6 percent last June.

   2. (about 6 percent) To indicate additional information.

3. The United States population increased from 3,929,214 in 1790 to 204,828,260 in 1970 U.S. Bureau of the Census.

   3. (U.S. Bureau of the Census). To enclose a reference.

4. McCready Bros. was founded in San Francisco in the early part of the twentieth century 1905.

   4. (1905). To indicate additional information.

5. Our district office staff consists of 1 the field manager, 2 seven technicians, and 3 two secretarial assistants.

   5. (1) . . . (2) . . . (3) With enumerating numbers in a list.

Other Punctuation Marks Used With Parentheses

When expressions enclosed in parentheses occur within sentences, no punctuation marks are used *before* the *opening* parenthesis, except in the case of enumerations. The closing parenthesis may be followed by any other mark of punctuation—comma, period, colon, and so on—called for by the sentence structure.

> **If you are ready for promotion (and I think you are), make application for the opening in Mr. Gray's office.** Note that there is no punctuation *before* the first parenthesis. A comma *follows* the closing one to set off an introductory clause.

> **The instructions are to insert the carbon pack in your typewriter (be sure the paper edges are even) and to start typing using a 5-inch line.** There is no punctuation before or after the parentheses in this sentence; punctuation is not used before, and the sentence structure calls for none after.

> **The advantages of our direct-mail service are these: (1) proven lists of customers, (2) greater market coverage, and (3) less cost to you.** Note that an enumeration is the only situation in which a mark of punctuation is used before an opening parenthesis; the colon introduces a list, and the comma separates the items in the list.

> **Does your firm handle office furniture—desks, chairs, file cabinets (all types)?** The whole sentence is a question; therefore, a question mark follows the closing parenthesis.

Note: The first word of a parenthetical expression within a sentence is not capitalized unless it is a proper noun, a proper adjective, the pronoun *I*, or the first word of a quoted sentence. When a parenthetical expression within a sentence requires end punctuation different from that of the sentence itself, the punctuation mark comes before the closing parenthesis.

> **Lawrence Perkins (isn't he now a successful lawyer?) was the youngest person to be graduated from this college.** The question mark applies only to the parenthetical material and therefore is placed before the closing parenthesis.

> **Anything flammable (books, papers, clothing, etc.) must be packed in these metal containers.** A period is required after the abbreviation *etc.*, which immediately precedes the closing parenthesis.

Parenthetical Sentences

Complete sentences may be enclosed in parentheses and allowed to stand by themselves. In this case, the first word of the sentence is capitalized, and the end punctuation is placed *before* the closing parenthesis. Remember that such complete parenthetical sentences are entirely independent, not part of another sentence.

> **There is no evidence of account discrepancies. (See the attached report for details.)** The parenthetical sentence is entirely separate and complete. The first word begins with a capital letter and the end period is placed *before* the closing parenthesis.

> **You are to be congratulated on your promotion. (How does it feel to be boss?)** The words in parentheses express a complete thought; in this case, a question. The question mark is placed *before* the closing parenthesis.

An important factor (perhaps the most important factor!) in her favor is that she has more than nine years' marketing experience. The exclamation point applies only to the material in parentheses and therefore is placed before the closing parenthesis.

Practice

Insert the punctuation marks called for in each of the following sentences, and capitalize where necessary.

1. Since you are acting supervisor (you surely will receive a full promotion soon) do you now attend the weekly production meeting

   1. **soon),...meeting?** Comma to set off introductory clause; question mark after question.

2. Please indicate your choice from the following entrees (they are the only ones available at the price quoted) roast beef chicken or ham.

   2. **quoted): roast beef, chicken,** Colon before a listing; commas between items in a series.

3. Order two reams of letterhead paper (is it 16- or 20-pound bond) for Mrs. Miller.

   3. **bond?)** Question mark belongs to parenthetical words and is placed inside ending parenthesis.

4. Mr. Keys could not answer your phone call (he was extremely busy today) but you will surely hear from him tomorrow.

   4. **today),** Compound sentence.

5. It is good practice to estimate your income and expenditures for a given period. (this is known as "budgeting")

   5. **(This . . . "budgeting.")** Parenthetical sentence. Period always is placed inside quotation marks.

6. Would you order 12 items at $5 apiece (regularly $6.98)

   6. **$6.98)?** The entire sentence is the question.

The Apostrophe

You have already studied the use of the apostrophe to indicate possession (see Unit 5) and to form plurals of letters, symbols, signs, and words used as words (see Unit 4). In Unit 20 you learned that the apostrophe can also be used as a single quotation mark. As a brief review, study the examples that follow.

> **Girls' and women's shoes will be on sale next week.** *Shoes belonging to girls and women*—the apostrophe indicates possession. See Unit 5 if you need help remembering why one apostrophe is *before* the *s*; the other, *after*.
>
> **Be sure to dot your *i*'s.** Apostrophe indicates the plural of the uncapitalized letter *i*.

Apostrophe Used in Contractions and Omission of Figures

An apostrophe is used to indicate a contraction—that is, a shortened form of a word.

don't *for* do not   o'clock *for* of the clock
doesn't *for* does not   nat'l *for* national
can't *for* cannot

An apostrophe is also used to show the omission of the first digits of a date, as in '77 for *1977*.

⚙ Practice

Practice the uses of the apostrophe by correctly punctuating the following sentences.

1. Denniss friend was hired today.

2. The "three Rs" will be the basis of our study.

3. He doesnt approve of the use of personal-size letterhead paper.

4. The Bicentennial celebration featured the Spirit of 76.

5. In some companies, employees birthdays are paid holidays.

6. Miss Kanes duties include okaying all invoices.

1. **Dennis's** Apostrophe and *s* are added to show possession.

2. **Correct** An apostrophe is not needed to form the plural of a *capital* letter.

3. **doesn't** To indicate a contraction.

4. **'76.** To indicate omission of figures.

5. **employees'** *Birthdays of employees.*

6. **Kane's** To show possession.

✖ Assignment

Check your ability to use parentheses and apostrophes correctly by doing Self-Check 21; then use the Self-Check Key to evaluate your work. In addition, complete Review Sheet 21, and turn it in to your instructor for scoring.

 # Capitalization

YOUR OBJECTIVE
To use capital letters correctly in proper nouns and in headings and titles.

REMEMBER . . .
Capital letters, as well as punctuation marks, are signals to help the reader understand your message easily and clearly.

A proper noun is the name of a particular person, place, or thing.

Two Basic Rules

Two basic, often-used principles of capitalization are ones you use automatically and will need only a brief review here.

1. The first word of a sentence is capitalized. A capital at the beginning of a sentence alerts the reader to the fact that a new thought is being expressed.
2. The personal pronoun *I* is always capitalized.

Names of Persons

A person's name is always capitalized—a principle that you already know. Some names with prefixes, however, need special study. The prefixes *O'* and *Mc* are followed by a capital letter without extra spacing: *O'Brien, McIntyre.* The prefix *Mac* may or may not be followed by a capital, depending on each person's preference: *MacNamara, Macmillan.* Make a special effort to write a name the way the person wants it written

Whether or not to capitalize the prefixes *d, da, de, della, di, du, la, le, lo, van* and *von* also depends on an individual's preference. Always check to see whether someone's name is *Jean duPont* or *Jean DuPont, Marie von Hatten* or *Marie VonHatten* or *Marie Von Hatten, Charles deFoe* or *Charles DeFoe,* since the capitalization and/or spacing may vary. However, when such a last name is used by itself (that is, without the first name), then capitalize the prefix.

Please ask *DuPont.*
Check that with *Von Hatten.*
It was written by *DeFoe.*

Names of Places

Capitalize names of states, cities, streets, parks, rivers, buildings, and other places.

> **Maine   Chicago   Main Street   Central Park   Mississippi River   Hill Building**

Capitalize points of the compass when they are used to denote a particular section of the country, not when they are used to denote a direction.

> **The Northeast is a popular summer vacation area.** *Northeast* is a *particular* section of the country.

> **We must drive northeast to reach Montreal from here.** In this sentence *northeast* is a direction, not a location; therefore, it is *not* capitalized.

Capitalize the word *city* only when it is part of the corporate name of the city.

> **Long Island City** (*but* the city of Milwaukee)

Capitalize the word *state* only when it follows the name of a state.

> **Indiana State** (*but* the state of Indiana)

Capitalize the word *the* in names of places only when *the* is a part of the official name.

> **One borough of New York City is The Bronx.** (*But* the Maritime Provinces.)

✐ Practice

In the following sentences, indicate which words should be capitalized. Be able to explain why.

1. When you travel to england, you will surely want to visit london.

   1. **England . . . London.** Names of geographical locations.

2. Their family name is la garza.

   2. **La Garza.** Capitalize the name prefix when only the last name is used.

3. The Nautilus traveled under the north pole.

   3. **North Pole.** A geographical location.

4. Mary o'connor is our new tax consultant.

   4. **O'Connor** Capitalize the prefix *O'* and the letter following the apostrophe.

5. The entire family will move to the south since Mr. von Patten has a new job.

   5. **South** A location, not a direction. The prefix *von* is correctly written.

6. In the Netherlands, you will enjoy visiting the Hague.

   6. **The Hague.** *The* is part of the official city name.

7. The triangle building is in the state of Illinois.

   7. **Triangle Building** Capitalize names of buildings. The word *state* is correctly written.

Names of Organizations and Trade Names

Capitalize the names of particular companies, associations, societies, commissions, committees, bureaus, boards, departments, schools, political parties, conventions, fraternities, clubs, religious bodies, and similar specific groups.

> **Our family belongs to the First Methodist Church.** *First Methodist Church* is capitalized because it is the name of a particular institution.
>
> **Our family attends the first church that was erected in this city.** Here *first church* is not the name of a particular institution; therefore, it is not capitalized.

The names of some organizations begin with *the*. When *the* is part of the official name, it should be capitalized. If you do not know whether *the* is a part of the official name, check to find out.

> **Do you have an account with The Detroit Bank and Trust Company?** *The* is included in the official title.
>
> **Miss LoPresti now works for the Child Welfare Committee.** *The* is not a part of the official title.

Not only are company names capitalized, but trade names of the products that they make are also capitalized.

> **A new product, Trimend, is made by the Smith Company.** *Trimend* is a trade name and is properly capitalized.
>
> **The new product, Trimend liquid cement, is made by the Smith Company.** Note that only the trade name is capitalized; the description of the product—*liquid cement*—is not capitalized.

Governmental Bodies, Historical Events, and Documents

Capitalize the names of countries and international organizations as well as national, state, county, and city bodies and their branches.

> **Dr. Stephen Day is employed by the Federal Bureau of Investigation.** The name of a particular government agency is capitalized.
>
> **Dr. Stephen Day turned the investigation over to a federal investigatory bureau.** In this sentence *bureau* is not capitalized because a *particular* agency has not been named.

Names of historical events and important documents are also capitalized. These include names of eras, specific treaties, bills, and laws: the *Stone Age*, *World War II*, the *Bill of Rights*, the *Constitution*, the *Social Security Act*.

Holidays

Names of holidays and other specific periods of time are capitalized: *New Year's Day, Christmas, National Education Week, Passover, Easter.* Note that the word *day* or *week* is capitalized when it is part of the name of the holiday.

⚙️ Practice

Apply the rules for capitalizing proper names in the following sentences.

1. Did you see the declaration of independence in independence hall?

1. **Declaration of Independence** Name of historical document.
   Independence Hall Name of a building.

2. The department of labor will send you the data required.

2. **Department of Labor** Name of a governmental agency.

3. You are invited to spend christmas day with our family.

3. **Christmas Day** Name of a holiday.

4. The United States army recruitment office is in the Bates Building.

4. **Army** Official name of a branch of service. *Bates Building* is correctly written.

5. What special activity is planned for senior citizens' week?

5. **Senior Citizens' Week?** A special week.

6. The baptist church is the only church in the community.

6. **Baptist Church** Only the name of the *particular* organization is capitalized.

7. Are you a member of the newly organized club, the humanity society?

7. **Humanity Society?** Name of a particular society.

In Letter Parts

In salutations the *first* word, titles, and names are capitalized: *Dear Mr. Bradley*, but *My dear Mr. Bradley*. In complimentary closings, only the *first* word is capitalized: *Very truly yours, Sincerely yours*, and so on.

Headings and Titles of Publications

In titles of manuscripts or publications, capitalize all words of four letters or more. In addition, capitalize all words of three letters or fewer *except* the following:

ARTICLES: *the, a, an*
SHORT CONJUNCTIONS: *and, as, but, if, or, nor*
SHORT PREPOSITIONS: *at, by, for, in, of, off, on, out, to, up*

The name of the book is *Teaching Principles and Procedures for Gregg Shorthand.* The words *and* and *for* are not capitalized.

Please read the article, "The Use of High-Speed Power Tools." The preposition *of* is not capitalized, but *the* is because it begins the sentence.

The poem, "Nature Through a Child's Eyes," will be published. The article *a* is not capitalized.

Always capitalize the first and last words of a title and the first word following a dash or colon in a title, even if these words are articles, short conjunctions, or prepositions. Also, in headings and titles capitalize each part of a hyphenated term.

> They are the authors of *How to Develop Effective Direct-Mail Advertising.* The second part of the hyphenated term *Direct-Mail* is hyphenated.
>
> The essay is titled, **"The World We Live In."** *In* is a short preposition, but it is correctly capitalized as the last word in the title.
>
> Study this report, **"Prospects for the Future: A Statistical Analysis."** *A* is correctly capitalized here following a colon within the title.

Proper Adjectives

Proper nouns are capitalized; also, most adjectives derived from proper nouns are capitalized. These are called *proper adjectives.*

> Ordinarily, **American people are considered to be generous.** *American* is a proper adjective derived from the proper noun *America.*
>
> Have you listened to the **Wagnerian operas?** *Wagnerian* is a proper adjective derived from the proper name *Wagner.*

Always check your dictionary if you are in doubt as to whether a proper adjective should be capitalized.

Nicknames

Sometimes a famous person or place is almost as well known by a nickname as by the real name. When a nickname is used in place of the name, it is capitalized.

> It is said that the **Great Emancipator** had a keen sense of humor. *Great Emancipator* is a descriptive term frequently used to refer to Lincoln and is used in place of his name in this sentence.
>
> The company offices are located in **The Loop.** *The Loop* is a common nickname for the downtown area of Chicago.

✪ Practice

In the following sentences, capitalize where necessary. Be able to give reasons for your choices.

1. Her new book, *the English-speaking nations,* will be published in the fall.

    1. *The English-Speaking Nations,* Book title.

2. Do you need a passport to cross the mexican border?

    2. **Mexican** Proper adjective.

3. I have studied your pamphlet, *how to invest and increase your holdings.*

    3. *How to Invest and Increase Your Holdings. To,* a short preposition, and *and,* a short conjunction, are not capitalized.

4. Purchase two copies of the book, *prosperity: a result of education.*

5. One look at tom's hair and you can see why we call him red.

6. Ms. Juarez always uses the complimentary closing *very sincerely yours.*

4. *Prosperity: A Result of Education.* Book title.

5. **Tom's, Red** *Tom* is a proper name; *Red* is a nickname.

6. **Very** Only the first word of a complimentary closing is capitalized.

Titles Used With Names of Persons

Titles are capitalized when they *precede* the name of a person; they are usually not capitalized when they *follow* or are used *in place of* a personal name.

> **Special messages were read from President Cook, Professor Harvey, and Baron Beaverton.** *President, Professor,* and *Baron* are correctly capitalized because they precede the names of people.
>
> **The chairperson, Mrs. Lucille Jankowski, city editor of the *Newton News*, called a committee meeting on Thursday.** *Mrs.* is a title preceding a name and is correctly capitalized. *City editor* is not capitalized for it *follows* the name.

Titles of *high* government officials are correctly capitalized when they follow or replace the person's name. This exception to the general rule includes the President and Vice President of the United States, cabinet officers, members of the United States Congress, state governors, and lieutenant governors.

> **Walter Mondale was elected Vice President in 1976.** Top government titles like *Vice President* are capitalized before or after the person's name.
>
> **Dwight D. Eisenhower, late President of the United States, was also president of Columbia University.** *President* here is capitalized in one place, not in the other (when it is not a top government position).
>
> **Miss Munoz is the youngest Representative in the House.** *Representative* and *House* are shortened forms referring to the United States House of Representatives.

Occasionally a title or word referring to a specific person or thing will be capitalized even when the actual name is not used. This is usually done when the writing is intended for limited readership and the writer and the reader are closely connected to the person or thing referred to.

> **This report should be sent to the Dean immediately.** Assuming that the reader knows the name of the person referred to; for example, *Dean Robertson.*
>
> **Did you have any idea you would be appointed to the Board?** *Board* can be correctly capitalized here as long as it means a particular one—*Board of Education, Board of Trustees*—known to the reader.

✸ Practice

Indicate which words should be capitalized in the following sentences. These sentences give practice in the writing of shortened names that refer to particular persons, places, and things.

1. Our association has given a $500 scholarship to a needy student.

1. **Correct** *Association* is a general term of classification; capitalization is not required.

2. The youngest member of the senate was appointed to a special committee.

2. **Senate** Refers to the *U.S. Senate; committee* is not capitalized because no particular committee is specified.

3. Our membership includes a judge, a professor, and a senator.

3. **Correct** These titles do not refer to particular persons.

4. Have you ever visited the state capital and gracie mansion?

4. **Gracie Mansion?** A specific building; *state capital* is not capitalized.

5. The governor of our state attended a meeting with several other state governors.

5. **Governor** Replaces a specific personal name; *governors* is a general term of classification and is not capitalized.

Hyphenated Titles

When *ex-* and *-elect* are joined to titles, they are not capitalized (except in headings and titles of works). Although not hyphenated, *former* and *late* are also not capitalized.

> Does ex-President Ford receive a pension from the government?
> The welcoming address will be given by Councilwoman-elect Ada Jones; the farewell, by John Weiss, the former Lieutenant Governor.

✐ Practice

In the following sentences, indicate which titles need to be capitalized.

1. A rigorous campaign was conducted by senator-elect West.

1. **Senator-elect** Title before a name.

2. Miss Jeanne McKenna, director of physical fitness, started a new health program.

2. **Correct** Titles following a name are not generally capitalized.

3. You recommended captain Bob Grant as chairman of the Officers' Advisory Committee.

3. **Captain** *Captain* is capitalized because it precedes the name; *chairman* follows the name and is not capitalized.

4. Ronald McKay, United States senator, recommended Andrew Abbate for Annapolis.

4. **Senator** High government positions are capitalized before and after a person's name.

5. No one recognized ex-mayor Stewart.

5. **ex-Mayor** Title preceding a name.

≉ Assignment

Check your ability to use capital letters correctly by doing Self-Check 22; then use the Self-Check Key to evaluate your work. In addition, complete Review Sheet 22, and turn it in to your instructor for scoring.

Abbreviations

YOUR OBJECTIVE
To use abbreviations in ways that are acceptable in business writing.

REMEMBER . . .
Whether words are written in full or abbreviated, the same rules of capitalization apply.

Use of Abbreviations

As a general rule, abbreviations are avoided in business writing. However, a number of abbreviations, such as those of titles and of names of some well-known associations, are commonly used and are acceptable. The principles discussed in this unit will aid you in deciding when and how to abbreviate.

Titles Before Names

The following principles govern the use of titles with names:

1. Always abbreviate the titles *Mr., Messrs., Mrs., Ms.,* and *Dr.* when they are written before either the complete name or the surname of a person.

Mr. Frank Aquilla	Messrs. Brown and Smith	Ms. Wanna Johnson
Mrs. Georgella Watts	Dr. Gregory Dario	

    Note: *Miss* and its plural form *Misses* are not abbreviations; therefore, they are not included in the above examples. The plural of *Ms.* is *Mses.* or *Mss.*

2. Spell out *Reverend* and *Honorable,* and always use *the* before each title. The abbreviations *Rev.* and *Hon.* may be used in less formal correspondence.

the Reverend William Plumb (*less formal:* Rev. William Plumb)
the Honorable Estelle Robb (*less formal:* Hon. Estelle Robb)

3. Spell out military titles. In less formal correspondence, long titles may be abbreviated.

   Captain Annette Newberry
   Lieutenant Commander John Mars (*less formal:* **Lt. Comdr. John Mars**)

4. Spell out all other titles.

Governor Buckle	**President Myrna Bresky**
Representative Pike	**Senator William Miron**

Titles After Names

The following rules govern the use of titles written *after* the name of a person:

1. Abbreviate such titles as *Junior (Jr.)* and *Senior (Sr.)* when they follow the name of a person.

Mr. Eldon Stein Jr.	**Randolph Lee III**
Mr. Raymond Brinson Sr.	**Damon Wentz 3d**

   Note that no comma is used between the person's name and the title of *Jr.* and *Sr.* or the roman and arabic numerals. However, some individuals prefer to use a comma between their name and such a title. The individual's preference should be followed whenever possible.

2. Abbreviations of religious orders, academic degrees, and so on, following a person's name are always separated with commas.

Andrew Wycoff, F.S.C.	**Agnes Brett, M.B.A., Ph.D., C.P.A.**
Helen Andretti, M.D.	**Anthony Bryzinski, D.D.S.**
Phillip Ager, Esq.	

   Note: *CPA* is generally written without periods. In the above example it is written *C.P.A.* only for consistency with *M.B.A.* and *Ph.D.* Also, note that the titles *Dr., Mr., Miss, Mrs.,* and *Ms.* are not used when such abbreviations follow a person's name.

Names of People

Abbreviations of first names, such as *Chas.* for *Charles, Jas.* for *James,* and *Wm.* for *William,* are not acceptable in business writing. Initials representing first and middle names are, of course, acceptable.

Names of Firms

A firm name should not be abbreviated unless the company itself uses an abbreviation. The best procedure is to check the company's letterhead to determine which words, if any, are abbreviated in the official name of the firm. Frequently the words *Company (Co.), Corporation (Corp.), Incorporated (Inc.),* and *Limited (Ltd.)* are abbreviated in firm names.

Gonzalez Foods Inc.   **Oulettes Ltd.**   **The Greenwood Paper Co.**

Note that there is no comma used in the preceding examples between the company name and the abbreviations *Inc.* and *Ltd.* The trend is to omit these commas. However, follow the company's preference when you know it.

⚙️ Practice

Indicate in the following sentences the words that should be abbreviated and those that should be spelled out.

1. Write to Prof. Groves for her booklet on procedures.

   1. **Professor**   Spelled out titles.

2. Captain Claude Walters made the decision immediately.

   2. **Correct**   Spell out titles.

3. A complete production schedule can be obtained from Mr. Chas. Evans.

   3. **Charles**   Never abbreviate a person's name.

4. A dr. was hired by the McFadden Corp. on a full-time basis.

   4. **doctor**   *Corp.* is correct if the company writes it that way; otherwise, it should be spelled out.

5. Reserve space on Flight 306 for the Reverend Harmon Gates.

   5. **Correct**   Spell out titles.

Names of Associations and Government Agencies

Probably because of the need to save time, abbreviations for names of associations are becoming more and more commonly used and are considered correct. If you use such abbreviations, be sure that they are in general use and will not be misunderstood by the reader. When the abbreviation consists of capital letters only, type it without periods or spaces.

NEA   National Education Association
SPCA   Society for the Prevention of Cruelty to Animals

The business of our government is conducted by many agencies whose abbreviated names are familiar to most people. These abbreviations are written without periods or spaces when they consist of capital letters only.

FBI   (Federal Bureau of Investigation)
SEC   (Securities and Exchange Commission)

A number of nongovernmental organizations also are well known by their abbreviated names. The best procedure is not to abbreviate unless you are certain your reader will immediately recognize the organization. Note that the following examples do not contain periods or spaces.

TWA (Trans World Airlines)
IBM (International Business Machines Corporation)
AFL-CIO (American Federation of Labor and Congress of Industrial Organizations)
NBC (National Broadcasting Company)

Although the call letters of radio and television stations are not abbreviations, you should remember that they are written in capital letters without periods or spaces; for example, *WNFC* and *WNFC-TV*.

Letters for Names

When a letter is used to designate a person or a thing, do not use a period after the letter; for example, *Mrs. K*, *Exhibit A*, and *Brand X*.

Chemical Symbols and Shortened Forms of Words

Do not use periods after chemical symbols. Also, do not use periods after shortened forms of words that are now considered complete words, not abbreviations.

Na (sodium)	**O** (oxygen)	**Fe** (iron)
ad (advertisement)	**gym** (gymnasium)	**phone** (telephone)

Contrary to popular belief, *IOU* and *SOS* are not abbreviations of words; therefore, these terms are not written with periods or spaces.

A.D., B.C., a.m., p.m.

When used with dates in historical reference, *anno Domini* (meaning "in the year of the Lord") and *before Christ* are always abbreviated *A.D.* and *B.C.* The abbreviation *B.C.* always follows the year. *A.D.* precedes the year.

20 B.C.   A.D. 1971

In expressions of time, the terms *ante meridiem* and *post meridiem* are always abbreviated *a.m.* and *p.m.* Remember, too, that these abbreviations are used only with figures and never with the word *o'clock*.

Please report at 9 *a.m.* *Or* nine o'clock in the morning.
Helen will leave *Tuesday afternoon.* Not *Tuesday p.m.*

Number

If the term *number* precedes a figure, as in a catalog number, write out *Number* if it is the first word in the sentence; otherwise, use the abbreviation *No.* (or its plural, *Nos.*). Note that the abbreviation is always capitalized. It is unnecessary to use *No.* with words like *Invoice, Check,* and so on.

Number 7480 should have been included in the order. Beginning of sentence.
Did you include *No.* 7480 in the order? Within the sentence.
Please make a copy of Invoice 8624. *No.* not needed.

Practice

In the following sentences, make the necessary corrections in abbreviation usage.

1. The plane departs at 6 o'clock p.m.

2. Ms. Fenway will visit the U. N. before returning to Los Angeles.

3. Julius Caesar was assassinated in B.C. 44.

4. The lab. assistant wrote the symbols Cl and Fe in his notes.

5. No. 23 is the item to be ordered.

1. **6 o'clock** *or* **6 p.m.** Do not use both *o'clock* and *p.m.*

2. **UN** Abbreviation of well-known organization; no periods or spaces.

3. **44 B.C.** B.C. always follows the year.

4. **lab** Considered a word; therefore, no period. The chemical symbols *Cl* (for chlorine) and *Fe* (for iron) are correct.

5. **Number** *Number* is written out at the beginning of a sentence.

Names of Cities

In business writing, write the names of cities in full. For example, write *Philadelphia,* not *Phila.; Los Angeles,* not *L.A.;* and *Chicago,* not *Chi.* However, abbreviate *Saint* in such city names as *St. Louis, St. Paul,* and *St. Petersburg.*

When they are used as part of city or other place names, always be sure to write *Fort, Mount, Point,* and *Port* in full; for example, *Fort Knox, Mount Whitney, Point Pleasant,* and *Port Huron.*

Names of States

The names of states should not be abbreviated when they are used in sentences. In addresses, lists, and so on, you may use either the traditional abbreviations (such as *Fla.* for *Florida* and *Mich.* for *Michigan*) or the newer two-letter abbreviations preferred in mailing addresses (such as *CA* for *California* and *MN* for *Minnesota*). See a reference manual for a complete listing of state abbreviations.

Names of Days and Months

Except in lists and tables where space is limited, do not abbreviate names of days of the week and months of the year. Never use an abbreviation for *May;* avoid the use of *Jun.* (for *June*) and *Jul.* (for *July*).

Points of the Compass

In general business writing, compass points such as *north, south, northeast,* and so on, are abbreviated only in addresses—specifically, only when they *follow* a street name to indicate a section of the city.

137 North 181st Street, *N.W.*

Note: In technical writing, compass-point abbreviations are written *without* periods: *NW, SE,* etc.

Street Names

Avoid using abbreviations for *street, avenue, road,* and so on, in all situations — especially when they are used in sentences.

Units of Measure

Units of measure — for example, *gallon, yard, pound, liter, meter, gram* — are generally spelled out. However, when they occur frequently or when they are used in tables, in lists, on business forms, or in nontechnical writing, units of measure are abbreviated.

IN BUSINESS WRITING	IN TABLES, ON BUSINESS FORMS, ETC.
a 2-gallon container	a 2-gal container
in 3-meter increments	in 3-m increments
two 25-pound cartons	two 25-lb cartons
approximately 5 grams	approximately 5 g

When abbreviating units of measure, always remember the following:

1. One abbreviation is used for both the singular and the plural: *gal* for *gallon* and *gallons; m* for *meter* and *meters;* etc.
2. Do *not* use periods after such abbreviations, as shown in the above examples.
3. Use numerals with units of measure unless the measurement has no technical significance.

   5 pounds *or* 5 lb   *But:* This package must weigh at least five pounds.

Check your dictionary or an authoritative reference manual for a complete list of abbreviations commonly used in business.

Plurals of Abbreviations

As you have seen, units of measure use the same abbreviation for both the singular and the plural. But most other abbreviations form their plurals by adding *s* to their singular forms:

No.	Nos.	CPA	CPAs
dept.	depts.	Ph.D.	Ph.D.s

Abbreviations that are made up of all-lowercase letters, however, generally use an apostrophe and *s* to form their plurals:

c.o.d.	c.o.d.'s
abc	abc's

Note: An exception is the abbreviation for *page:* its singular is *p.,* but its plural is *pp.*

✔ Practice

In the following sentences, indicate those words that should be spelled out.

1. Mr. Young's itinerary includes a two-day stop in Det., Mich.

2. Is the correct address 1557 W. State St.?

3. We will stay in Ft. Lauderdale for a week.

4. Our appointment is scheduled for Tues., Jan. 26.

5. Order at least 13 ms more of this fabric.

1. **Detroit, Michigan.** Do not abbreviate city names; avoid abbreviating state names in sentences.

2. **West State Street?** Abbreviate compass points only when they *follow* street names; avoid abbreviating *street.*

3. **Fort Lauderdale** Do not abbreviate *Fort* in a city name.

4. **Tuesday, January 26.** Avoid abbreviating days and months.

5. **13 m** *or* **13 meters** Do not add *s* to form the plural of abbreviations of units of measure.

✖ Assignment

Check your ability to use abbreviations in acceptable business style by doing Self-Check 23; then use the Self-Check Key to evaluate your work. In addition, complete Review Sheet 23, and turn it in to your instructor for scoring.

Numbers

YOUR OBJECTIVE
To choose correctly between numerals or spelled-out numbers, as appropriate according to modern business usage.

REMEMBER . . .
Properly used marks of punctuation and capital letters, as well as correct grammar and sentence structure, help the reader to understand the written word easily and clearly.

General Rules for Number Usage

Numbers are always written in figures in tables, charts, invoices, and other tabulated materials. However, in business letters, reports, memos, and so on, numbers may be written in words or in figures. Since numbers written in figures stand out and are easy to read and comprehend, most business writers prefer to spell out the numbers *1* through *10* (except when emphasis is needed, as in this sentence) and to use figures for numbers above 10. The general rule for writing numbers in ordinary business correspondence is: *Write the numbers* 1 *through* 10 *in words and use figures for all other numbers.*

> **Miss Waring worked for *three* years in the accounting department and for *ten* years in the marketing department.**
>
> **We would like to send you the *150* copies that you requested, but we have only *11* copies of the brochure in stock.**

Most of the rules discussed in the following paragraphs are exceptions to this general rule.

Number at Beginning of Sentence

A number that occurs at the beginning of a sentence is always written in words.

> **Two thousand stockholders voted against the proposal.**
> ***Thirty-two* patients requested flu shots.**

However, avoid beginning a sentence with a number that requires more than two words; for example, *one hundred and twenty-two*. Try to rewrite such sentences.

Ages of Persons

An age given in years only is written in words unless it is used as a significant statistic (as in a news release or in copy pertaining to employment), in which case it is written in figures.

> **Mr. Harris is *thirty-eight* years old.** Not a significant statistic, therefore, the number is written in words.
>
> **Our employees must retire at the age of *65*, but they may retire earlier.** A significant statistic.

An age given in years and months or in years, months, and days is always written in figures.

> **His youngest daughter is *4 years 11 months 12 days* old.** Note that commas are not used to separate the year-month-day unit.

Fractions and Mixed Numbers

A fraction without a whole number before it is expressed in words in ordinary business writing. A hyphen is used between the numerator and the denominator unless either element already contains a hyphen.

two-thirds (for ⅔)   five thirty-seconds (for ⁵⁄₃₂)

Polls indicate that the incumbent mayor will be reelected by a *two-thirds* majority. *Two-thirds* is a fraction without a whole number.

***Three-fourths* of the voters went to the polls in November.** *Three-fourths* is a fraction that should be hyphenated.

Write a mixed number (a whole number plus a fraction) in figures—except, of course, at the beginning of a sentence.

She spent 1½ hours addressing invitations, not 2¾ hours as she had estimated. Both figures are mixed numbers and are correctly written as figures.

Clock Time

When using the abbreviations *a.m.* and *p.m.*, always use figures to express time. A colon and zeros (*:00*) are not needed to show "on the hour" times except in tables where other times are given in hours and minutes.

The flight was scheduled to leave O'Hare at 2:45 p.m., but the plane did not leave until 3 p.m.

When using the word *o'clock*, use figures for emphasis (7 *o'clock*) or words for formality (*seven o'clock*).

Centuries and Decades

Numbers designating centuries may be expressed in either of these styles:

The company was founded in the *1800s. Or* the eighteen hundreds.
Much progress has been made in the *twentieth century.*

Decades may be expressed in any of the ways illustrated below.

the 1970s   the nineteen-seventies   the seventies   the '70s

⚙ Practice

In the following sentences, correct any errors in the writing of numbers.

1. At the age of 62, an employee may retire.

   1. **Correct** Significant statistic.

2. We should leave before 11:00 a.m.

   2. **11 a.m.** Omit *:00* for "time on the hour."

3. Only 7 people attended the meeting.

   3. **seven** Not a significant statistic; follow general rule for numbers *1* through *10*.

4. 275 ballots were cast in the last election.

   4. **In the last election, 275** Avoid such numbers at beginning of sentence.

5. We drove for 4½ hours.

   5. **Correct** Mixed number written in figures.

6. Her daughter is 11 years four months old.

   6. **11 years 4 months** Use figures for age in years and months.

7. That style was typical of the '50s.

7. **Correct** *The fifties* or the *1950s* or *the nineteen-fifties* also would be correct.

Amounts of Money

Amounts of money are written in figures. In writing a whole-dollar amount, omit the *.00* except in tables or charts containing dollar-and-cents amounts.

The price is *$49.95* plus local sales tax of *$3.*

Your March 5 order included these items:

1 Dress	$19.95
1 Blouse	4.98
1 Skirt	12.00

Except in tables, and so on, write isolated amounts of cents in figures with the word *cents.*

You can buy a good eraser for *25 cents.*

Addresses

With the exception of *One,* write house numbers in figures. In writing numbers used as street names, write the numbers *One* through *Ten* in words and all other numbers in figures. Always write ZIP Code numbers in figures.

She lives at *One* Park Avenue and has an office at *100* Center Street.

The correct address is as follows: Mr. Harold Nelson, 1400 North Tenth Street, Chicago, Illinois *60620.*

As illustrated below, numbered street names over *10* are commonly written without the ordinal endings *st, d* (or *nd* and *rd*), or *th.*

The store is at 2408 West 22 Street. *Or* 22d *or* 22nd.

Remember that commas are not used in house and ZIP Code numbers.

Related Numbers

Use the same style for all related numbers in a sentence—that is, write them all in figures or all in words. (Use figures if any number is above *10.*)

Please order *4* tables, *16* chairs, and *24* file cabinets. Note that two of the three numbers are over *10.*

We returned *one* table, *four* chairs, and *twelve* file cabinets. Only one of these three numbers is over *10.*

Adjacent Numbers

When two unrelated numbers appear together, write one of the numbers in figures and the other in words. The number that will make the shorter word is usually written out.

We need *12 six*-foot extension cords.
In *1971 sixteen* sales representatives were hired.

If two large numbers appear together, write both of them in figures and use a comma to separate them.

In *1960, 64,020,000* persons were employed throughout the United States.

Numbers in the Millions or Higher

Numbers in the millions or higher are often written in a combination of figures and words. However, a very large number that consists of more than a whole number plus a simple fraction or decimal must be written in figures.

12,500,000 *or* **12½ million** *or* **12.5 million**

As you see in the report, employment in the metropolitan area now stands at **3,256,850**. This number cannot be expressed as a whole number plus a simple fraction or decimal; therefore, it is written entirely in figures.

Practice

Correct the errors in number usage in the following sentences.

1. In 1970 314 employees were hired to expand the sales force.

1. **1970, 314**   Note the comma between the two unrelated numbers.

2. The letter was mailed to the following address: 12329 Wentworth Avenue, Detroit, Michigan 48,239.

2. **48239**   No comma in a ZIP Code number.

3. One order specified one hundred twenty-six 10-foot beams.

3. **126 ten-foot**   The smaller number is written out.

4. Is the correct amount $25.00 or $2.50?

4. **$25**   Omit *.00* in a whole-dollar amount.

5. She interviewed six sales representatives, eight secretaries, and 12 typists.

5. **twelve**   Related numbers, most of which are under *10*.

Indefinite Amounts

Indefinite amounts, such as *a few hundred* and *several thousand,* are always expressed entirely in words.

We mailed *several thousand* copies of the brochure. Not *several 1,000.*

Percentages

Except in tabulated material, write percentages in figures and use the word *percent,* not the symbol %.

The note was for $600 for 90 days at *7 percent* interest.
A *2 percent* discount will be given if payment is made within 10 days.

Note that all numbers used in quoting interest or discount rates and in related periods of time are expressed in figures.

Dates

In business writing, never use a figure to represent the month; for example, write *June* (not 6). Always write the day in figures without an ordinal ending when it follows the month. Always write the year in figures.

June 1   May 22
The invoice was dated *September 20, 1976.* Not 9/20/76.

When the day precedes the name of the month, it may be expressed either in ordinal figures (*1st, 2d, 3d, 4th,* and so on) or in ordinal words (*first, second, third, fourth,* and so on).

The office will close early on the *twenty-fourth* of December. *Or for added emphasis:* 24th of December.
Does your vacation begin the *third? Or for added emphasis:* 3d *or* 3rd.

◊ Practice

Correct the errors in number usage in the following sentences.

1. Is 9% a reasonable interest rate?   1. 9 percent

2. Over 3,000,000 people are now employed   2. 3 million
   in this metropolitan area.

3. The conference began March 4th.   3. March 4

4. Payment is due on the sixth of each month. 4. Correct *or* 6th

5. What is the interest on $300.00 for 60 days 5. $300
   at 6 percent?

❧ Assignment

Check your ability to write numbers correctly by doing Self-Check 24; then use the Self-Check Key to evaluate your work. In addition, complete Review Sheet 24, and turn it in to your instructor for scoring.

Effective Business Letters

YOUR OBJECTIVE
To apply basic and accepted business letter-writing techniques to create effective messages; to know the different parts of a business letter.

REMEMBER . . .
Being correct in the usage of grammar, punctuation, and other English-usage principles is a fundamental part of effective writing.

Business Writing

Business writing encompasses a variety of forms—letters, memorandums, reports, minutes of meetings, news releases—each with special characteristics. This unit will provide basic information about the most common form of business writing—the business letter.

Letters as Sales Agents

A business letter is always written for a specific purpose. For example, the writer's purpose may be to sell an idea or a product, to place an order, to get information, to collect a past-due account, or to ask for a job. Whatever the writer's primary purpose, a secondary purpose is to make a favorable impression on the reader. The writer must be able to sell his or her ideas by means of the written word. A letter is effective if it achieves the desired results; for example, a collection letter is effective if it results in a customer's paying an overdue account.

Characteristics of Effective Letters

Letters that produce the desired results have a number of characteristics in common. These characteristics are indicated in the following checklist, which you may want to use to evaluate the letters you write.

1. Does it look attractive on the page?
2. Is it correct in every detail?
3. Is it clear, concise, and complete?
4. Is it sincere, friendly, and tactful?
5. Does the letter use acceptable, modern terminology?

Attractive Appearance

At first glance, the reader is either favorably or unfavorably impressed by the overall appearance of a letter. A first impression will usually be favorable if the letter is placed attractively on the page, if the typing is even, with no strikeovers or obvious corrections, and if the letter is arranged in an acceptable letter style.

The last part of this unit provides a guide to common punctuation and arrangement styles for business letters.

Correctness in Detail

Errors of fact, although generally unintentional, can prevent a letter from accomplishing its purpose. To avoid factual errors, you need to recognize their common causes. One source of error is carelessness, such as transposing figures, failing to proofread accurately, making typographic mistakes that destroy readability, or omitting essential information. Another source of error is guessing at information, which often results in incorrect dates, figures, or word choices or in misspelled words and names (it is especially important to spell names correctly). Errors in punctuation sometimes change the meaning of a sentence.

Clear, Concise, and Complete Messages

An effective business letter combines completeness in detail with clear and concise writing. It is obvious that a message from which a necessary detail is omitted is not clear; unfortunately, it is sometimes not so obvious that a writer's words and the way they are used might not convey the message intended. In general, a writer should use simple, everyday expressions the reader will easily understand.

The expeditious dispatch of your check in the amount of $105.42 will be deemed to discharge all indebtedness to this firm. The long words that take the place of short, common ones (that is, *expeditious* for *quick*) and the unnecessary words (that is, *in the amount of* for *for*) tend to obscure the meaning of the sentence.

Your check for $105.42 will clear your account. It is much easier to understand this sentence than the first example. The long words have been replaced with simple, everyday words, and the unnecessary words have been eliminated.

A concise letter—a letter that covers the entire subject in the fewest possible words—is more certain to convey the message correctly than a rambling, wordy letter. However, guard against thinking that *concise* and *brief* mean the same thing; brevity is only a part of conciseness. To be concise, a message must be both complete *and* brief—but not so brief as to seem discourteous.

Your order reached us last week. It will be filled within the next month or two. This letter is brief, but it lacks courtesy and tact.

Thank you for your February 10 order for lawn furniture. Please be assured that you will receive shipment well before the May 10 deadline that you have set for your spring sale. This message takes more words than the previous example, but its positive and courteous tone helps to keep the customer's goodwill toward your firm.

What information is needed to make the following sentences clear? Can words be eliminated?

1. I need to know, at least I would like to know, the model number of your best-quality 10-inch stereo speaker.

2. Please send me a blouse advertised in to-day's *News*.

3. Please meet me this Friday.

4. We are sending our Memory Collection cassette tape recording; please send payment immediately.

5. We wish to acknowledge receipt of your letter of June 10 and thank you for same.

---

1. Replace unnecessary verbiage—*I need to know, at least I would like to know*—with **What is . . . .**

2. Size, color, and style are missing—**Please send me one Style B blouse, yellow, Size 32, which was advertised on page 4 of the March 21 edition of the *News*.**

3. What time? Where? **Please meet me in my office on Friday, March 10, at 10 a.m.**

4. How much does it cost? **We are sending our Memory Collection cassette tape recording, priced at $9.95 . . . .**

5. Why the extra words? **Thank you for your June 10 letter.**

Sincere, Friendly, and Tactful Messages

The wish to be appreciated and to be treated courteously is a very human trait. Letters are more likely to be received well if these two desires are considered. Saying *thank you* for a favor done and *please* for a favor requested are good ways to make and keep friends; however, the words of courtesy by themselves fall short of the desired effect if they are not a part of a total message that sounds sincere. *All* the words you choose must make the reader feel that you are interested and concerned.

> We cannot grant credit for your purchase. We grant credit only to those customers whose annual purchases exceed $1,000. We can't go to the expense of checking credit ratings for the small customer. Sorry. This example does not sound very friendly. The tone of the letter is *negative;* the word *sorry* does not sound as if the writer really *cares* about the reader.

> The considerable savings that we offer on cash orders are especially designed for customers like you, who have moderate-volume accounts. It is our regular policy, however, to extend credit only on accounts of $1,000 or more a year. This more positive example begins by stating the advantages to the cash customer and thus emphasizes the reader's point of view. The credit policy is explained clearly and tactfully, without belittling the reader; the entire tone is businesslike but friendly.

◆ **Practice**

Try to make the following sentences more sincere, friendly, and tactful. Be concerned with the reader's interests.

1. I didn't send your order out until yesterday. Sorry.

2. We can't make an exception for you in this case; our policy is firm.

3. You have no right to be upset, for we couldn't help the fact that our service representative failed to correct the difficulty with your washer.

4. We have too much money in payment of your last invoice. What should we do?

1. Please accept my apology for the delay in sending your order.

2. We would like to make an exception in this case; however, our policy is firm.

3. Thank you for telling us about the continuing difficulty with your washer. Our service representative will make the additional repairs without delay.

4. Your check dated September 19 for $25 was an overpayment of $2 on your account. Shall we credit the extra $2 to your account?

Modern Expressions

Some business people use old-fashioned expressions when they write letters. Such out-of-date expressions are avoided by the modern writer.

I beg to advise you that your account is long past due. *Beg to advise* is not a modern expression. This expression can be omitted and the sentence would read: *Your account is long past due.*

Herewith is my check in the amount of $25. *Herewith* and *in the amount of* are unnecessary words. Modern writers would simply say, *Here is* my check for $25.

Did you note in the previous examples that the modern expressions are direct and sound the way people talk? They are standard English, not words and phrases put together to make a peculiar letter-writing jargon.

Practice

Eliminate the old-fashioned terms in the following sentences, and substitute modern words or phrases.

1. I have before me your order of October 3.

2. Attached hereto is the report you requested in yesterday's meeting.

3. Your order will be sent by parcel post as per your instructions.

4. We state herewith that all employees are cordially invited to attend.

5. Our requisition was sent under date of May 20.

1. I have received your October 3 order.

2. Attached is the report you requested in yesterday's meeting.

3. Your order will be sent by parcel post, as you requested.

4. All employees are cordially invited to attend.

5. Our requisition was sent on May 20.

Letter Parts

Most business letters include *all* the following parts:

1. *The Heading.* The heading of a letter is the name, address, and phone number of the company. When this information is printed on stationery, that stationery is called *letterhead.* For example, see the letterhead for Early Bird Warning Systems and for Thompson Temporaries (illustrated on pages 131 and 135).

2. *The Date Line.* Every letter should include the date on which the letter was typed. In business letters the date line is typed in the following style: *January 12, 1978* (not *1/12/78*).

3. *The Inside Address.* The inside address usually includes the name of the person to whom you are writing, his or her title, the name of the company, the address of the company, and the city, state, and ZIP Code number. In the following examples of inside addresses, note that the addressee's name is preceded by a courtesy title such as *Mr., Mrs.,* etc.

Mr. John Aliano, President
Warwick Furniture Company Inc.
174 Tuller Drive
Milwaukee, WI 53254

Ms. Eleanor Grossman
Vice President, Finance
Younger and Cole, Publishers
17 Fifth Avenue
New York, New York 10017

4. *The Salutation.* The salutation is a greeting to the person or persons to whom you are writing. Here are some examples of some commonly used salutations:

SINGULAR FORM	PLURAL FORM	USE
Dear Bill: Dear Nikki:		Used for informal business correspondence – implies a personal friendship.
Dear Mr. Kraus: Dear Mr. Robb: Dear Ms. Balkan: Dear Mrs. Van Pelt:	Dear Messrs. Kraus and Robb: Dear Mmes. Balkan and Van Pelt	Used in routine business correspondence addressed to one or several individuals – formal but cordial.
	Ladies and Gentlemen: Gentlemen: Ladies:	Used for correspondence addressed to a company or to a group.
Dear Madam: Dear Sir: Dear Madam or Sir: Madam: Sir: Madam or Sir:	Dear Mesdames: Dear Sirs: Dear Mesdames or Sirs: Mesdames: Sirs: Mesdames or Sirs:	Used only for formal correspondence.

5. *The Body.* Obviously, the body, or message, is the most important part of the letter. As you will see on pages 132 and 133, the body of the letter may include a subject line, which gives the reader advance notice of what the letter is all about. Generally, the body of the letter should include at least two paragraphs.

Early Bird WARNING SYSTEMS
275 Carlton Street, Long Beach, CA 90840

May 22, 1977

Mr. John T. Wentworth
3428 Royal Palm Boulevard
Palm Springs, CA 90804

Dear Mr. Wentworth:

SUBJECT: MAKING YOUR HOME SAFE

Many thanks for calling us yesterday. We treat every call as an act of trust in our service. Therefore, we pledge the most up-to-date methods of home protection from fire and theft.

As you requested, we shall arrive at your home at 2 p.m. on Wednesday, May 31, to give you our complimentary safety check. We shall show you several ways in which you can make your home safe for you and your family. There are probably some things we can suggest that you can easily do yourself for little or no money. The items that call for installation with our equipment and expertise will be described to you. Then we shall mail you an estimate for our work plus full descriptive literature. You will be under no obligation. You may select all or part of the items we suggest. We can also arrange an easy payment plan.

Sincerely,

EARLY BIRD WARNING SYSTEMS

Hazel T. Reddick

Ms. Hazel T. Reddick
Sales Manager

tco

Enclosure

cc Wesley J. Martin

6. *The Complimentary Closing.* Just as the salutation says "Hello," the complimentary closing says "Goodbye." Thus the tone of the complimentary closing should match the tone of the salutation. It would be obviously ridiculous to match a salutation such as *Dear Joan* with a complimentary closing such as *Very sincerely yours.* Here are some commonly used complimentary closings.

FORMAL	INFORMAL
Yours very truly,	Sincerely.
Very truly yours,	Cordially,
Very sincerely yours,	Sincerely yours,
Very cordially yours,	Cordially yours,
Respectfully yours,	Best regards,

7. *The Signature Block.* The signature block includes the writer's signature, followed by the writer's typewritten name and job title (and/or department).

Maria P. Carmichael, Director

Jack F. DeLorenzo
Manager, Credit Department

Some companies prefer using a *company signature* immediately after the complimentary closing. See page 131 for an example.

8. *The Reference Initials.* Because it is frequently important to know who typed a specific letter, reference initials (the initials of the person who typed the letter) are generally included in business letters. The reference initials may also include the initials of the person who wrote the letter; when they do, the initials of the person who wrote the letter are typed *before* the initials of the person who typed the letter. Here are some commonly used styles for typing reference initials:

JST:eh   WAS/jb   PRV:JN

In addition to the eight letter parts described above, there are some optional letter parts, one or more of which may be used in a particular business letter.

9. *The Attention Line.* Sometimes a letter is addressed to a company or to a department within a company rather than to a specific person. In such cases, an attention line is used. As you see below, the attention line is typed in all-capital letters or in underscored capital and lowercase letters.

ATTENTION MS. LYNDA CLARK
ATTENTION ACCOUNTING DEPARTMENT
Attention Ms. Lynda Clark
Attention Accounting Department

Note: When using an attention line, always use one of the following salutations: *Gentlemen:* or *Ladies:* or *Ladies and Gentlemen:*.

10. *The Subject Line.* When a writer wants to give the reader advance notice of what the letter is about, he or she does so by including a subject line. The subject is always included directly *below the salutation,* so that it acts as a heading. Like the attention line, the subject line may be typed

in all-capital letters or in underscored capital and lowercase letters. The word *Subject* may be omitted, but when it is included, it is always followed by a colon:

SUBJECT: LEASE RENEWAL
Subject: Lease Renewal

11. *The Enclosure Notation.* Whenever something is included with the letter in the same envelope or package, an enclosure notation must be used. This notation tells the reader that something has been included with the letter. It also reminds the secretary that something must be included with the letter. Obviously, such a notation is very helpful on a file copy of the letter. Enclosure notations are generally typed as follows:

Enclosure	Enclosures
Enc.	1. Check
Enclosures (2)	2. Memo
Enc. (2)	3. Envelope

12. *The Mailing Notation.* When the letter is sent by some special service, such as *certified mail* or *special delivery,* this special service should be noted on all copies of the letter. The mailing notation should be typed below the reference initials (or below any enclosure notations). See, for example, the mailing notation shown in the letter on page 135.

13. *Carbon Copy Notation.* A carbon copy (*cc*) notation is typed on the original and all duplicate copies of the letter to show that a copy has been sent to a specific person or persons.

  A blind carbon (*bcc*) notation is never typed on the original copy of the letter; it is typed only on the copies. Notice the styles generally used for typing *cc* and *bcc* notations:

cc Mr. Henry Aaron	CC Ms. F. Woods	bcc Mr. Jonathan Todd
cc: Mrs. Helen Luzinski	CC: Ms. Abby Grant	bcc: Dr. Oscar Campbell

14. *The Postscript (PS).* A *PS* may be added to the bottom of the letter for either of two purposes: (1) to add something that the writer has forgotten to include in the message or (2) to emphasize something by drawing the reader's attention to it.

Punctuating Letter Parts

The body—the message part—of a business letter is punctuated using, of course, the standard rules of punctuation. In a business letter, the salutation and the complimentary closing are treated specially. Usually the complimentary closing ends with a comma, and the salutation ends with a colon:

Dear Dr. Rifkin:	Sincerely yours,
My dear Reverend Sawyer:	Very truly yours,
Dear Miss Francoise:	Cordially,

All other display lines in a business letter end in no punctuation—unless, of course, the line ends in an abbreviation such as *Inc., Ltd., Jr.,* or *enc.* See the examples illustrated on pages 135–137.

Styles of Business Letters

The parts of a business letter may be arranged—that is, placed on the page—in different ways. The most commonly used letter styles, called the *blocked,* *semiblocked,* and *full-blocked* styles, are described and illustrated on the following pages. In each illustration, note that the body is typed single-spaced and that a blank line is used between paragraphs.

Blocked Letters

The blocked style is widely used in business today. The date line is centered. Each line of the inside address begins at the left margin, as do all paragraphs. The body of the letter is single-spaced, with double spacing between paragraphs. The complimentary closing and the signature block begin at the center of the page. See the example on page 135.

Semiblocked Letters

The semiblocked letter is exactly like the blocked letter *with one exception:* paragraphs are indented five spaces. See the example on page 136.

Full-Blocked Letters

The full-blocked letter saves typing time because the typist does not need to use the tabular key. Each line, including the date line, starts at the left margin. The body of the letter is single-spaced, with double spacing between paragraphs. (If the body of the letter were double-spaced, there would be no way to distinguish between paragraphs.) See the example on page 137.

🎶 Practice

If any of the following statements are false, can you change the information so that the statement will be true?

1. In a full-blocked letter, every line *except* the date line begins at the left margin.

   1. **False**   Every line *including* the date line.

2. Most business letters are single-spaced, with double spacing between paragraphs.

   2. **True**

3. A date line may be omitted to save space in a long letter.

   3. **False**   A date line must always be included.

4. A comma is used after a salutation, and a colon is used after a complimentary closing.

   4. **False**   The opposite is true.

✂️ Assignment

Check your ability to write letters in acceptable business form by doing Self-Check 25; then use the Self-Check Key to evaluate your work. In addition, complete Review Sheet 25, and turn it in to your instructor for scoring.

893 South Loop, Atlanta, GA 30312

March 19, 19--

Ms. Eloise Benoit
Benoit and Guidry Ltd.
3555 Kensington Avenue
Ottawa, Ontario
CANADA K1P 5J6

Dear Ms. Benoit:

This blocked letter style is still very popular for two reasons:

1. Many people feel comfortable with the traditional
    appearance.

2. The blocked paragraphs make it slightly more effi-
    cient to type.

Lists, quotations, and addresses may be indented on either side
for a clearer display. If it is necessary to use more than one
paragraph for a quotation, a standard single blank line is left
between paragraphs.

Special mail service, such as special delivery or registered
mail, is shown on the line below the reference initials. We do
so only to record this information for our files.

When the letter is being sent to a foreign address, the country
is typed in all-capital letters on a separate line, as CANADA is
shown above.

                    Sincerely yours,

                    Jasper F. Broussard
                    Jasper F. Broussard
                    Senior Account Executive

urs
Registered

PS. We treat postscripts in the same way that we treat other
paragraphs, except that we precede each postscript by PS: or
PS.

thompson temporaries

893 South Loop, Atlanta, GA 30312

March 19, 19--

Byrd, Cointreau, and Terry Inc.
2085 Mandell Parkway
Fort Worth, TX 76111

ATTENTION TRAINING DIRECTOR

Ladies and Gentlemen:

The semiblocked letter is still popular because of its
traditional appearance. The indented paragraphs give this style
a distinctive look.

This letter also shows an alternative arrangement for the
attention line: centered, in all capitals (instead of being
blocked at the left margin and underscored). In two respects,
however, the use of the attention line here is standard: it
is accompanied, as it should be, by a salutation, Ladies and
Gentlemen, and it is typed above the salutation.

Worth noting also in this letter are the following:
(1) positioning the date at the center as an alternative to
ending it at the right margin; (2) using standard punctuation,
which calls for a colon after the salutation and a comma after
the complimentary closing; and (3) using the carbon copy notation at the bottom to indicate to whom copies of the letter are
being sent.

Cordially yours,

Jasper F. Broussard

Jasper F. Broussard
Senior Account Executive

urs
cc Ms. J. Laver
   Dr. T. Mauser

893 South Loop, Atlanta, GA 30312

June 10, 19--

Ms. Susan B. Audobon
Gulf Coast Consumers Inc.
2425 Slidell Road
New Orleans, LA 20511

Dear Ms. Audobon:

Subject: Form of a Full-Blocked Letter

This letter style is fast becoming the most popular style in
use today. Efficiency is the main reason for its popularity.
The typist can save time and eliminate the necessity of working
out placement. Some organizations are even designing letterheads
to accommodate this style. A few years ago, some people felt
the full-blocked style looked odd. That complaint is seldom
heard today, however. As more organizations use a full-blocked
style, people have become accustomed to its appearance.

This letter also illustrates one arrangement of the subject line
that may be used with any style of letter. Like an attention
line, a subject line may be typed with underscores or in capitals.
In a full-blocked letter, it must be blocked; in other letter
styles, it may be blocked or centered. It always appears after
the salutation and before the body, for it is considered a part
of the body.

Sincerely,

Jasper F. Broussard

Jasper F. Broussard
Senior Account Executive

urs
Enclosure

Index